****ASK YOURSELF THESE QUESTIONS****

DO YOU . . .

- Let other people influence what you do, say, and feel about yourself?
- Imagine a constantly hostile "out there" environment?
- Harbor loads of guilt?
- Smoke, drink too much, or use drugs?
- Have no significant relationships with other people?
- Let others walk all over you?
- Dwell on disaster?
- Swallow your anger?

IF THE ANSWER IS "YES," READ ON. . . .

By Megan LeBoutillier
Published by Ballantine Books:

LITTLE MISS PERFECT
"NO" IS A COMPLETE SENTENCE

"NO" IS A COMPLETE SENTENCE

Megan LeBoutillier

BALLANTINE BOOKS • NEW YORK

Copyright © 1995 by Megan LeBoutillier

All rights reserved under International and Pan-American Copyright Conventions. Published in the United States by Ballantine Books, a division of Random House, Inc., New York, and simultaneously in Canada by Random House of Canada Limited, Toronto.

Library of Congress Catalog Card Number: 94-96481

ISBN 0-345-37647-1

Printed in Canada

First Edition: April 1995

10 9 8 7 6 5 4

The use of the male pronoun throughout this work is intended merely to offer simpler and more consistent reading.

Dedicated to:

Alexandra and Tim,
my dearest friends,
who taught me what healthy boundaries could be

Contents

        ix

Contents

Acknowledgments

To all the people who have passed through my life, bearing either understanding or intrusion, I say thank you for contributing to my learning adventure concerning personal boundaries.

Thank you to Betsy Vonk for first turning attention toward the subject; to Judith Reineck, Kathy McGrogan, Carol Winans, Kay Scott and Christine Thomas, for reading my work in progress and letting me test out my ideas. A special thanks to everyone who shared their story with me.

Thanks to Cheryl Woodruff, for liking the idea, and Cathy Repetti, for her help and patience.

Introduction

I HAVE AN ANXIOUS MEMORY FROM CHILDHOOD THAT RE-
volves around a game we played during physical educa-
tion classes on rainy days. The game was called
"bombardment," and for me it was a game of terror.

The spirit of competition was set by two opposing
teams formed through the painful ordeal of "picking
sides." Self-esteem began eroding as names were called,
but not yours. Everyone has a memory like this—the
pain of not being chosen. Then there was the game itself.

The purpose of the game was to throw a pink ball as
hard as you could into the throng of the other team and
hit someone—hard. Once hit, that person became a prisoner and had to retreat to a thin space behind the other
team, outlined by the end zone of the basketball court.
In prison the player had to yell and scream to her team-

mates, begging them to forgo taking a hostage and throw the ball instead over everyone's head so that she could catch it. If this move succeeded, the lucky prisoner could then use the ball to free herself by once again hurling it with great force into the stomach, chest, or thigh of the enemy.

It was a vicious game. I hated it. I would feel nervous until I was finally taken prisoner. I wanted to run right out front so that I was sure to be hit, just to escape the anxiety. Once in prison, I could relax a bit until a well-meaning friend would send me the ball, and then I was back into the skirmish and the fear.

Over the years I have thought about this game many times. It has become a metaphor of human behavior for me. Oversimplified, perhaps, but the ideas of competition, bombardment, aggression, anxiety, relief from anxiety, and imprisonment are all tied together for me in a question about the relationship between personal boundary violation and acts of self-harm. I wonder about my wish to sacrifice myself at the start of the game just to avoid the feelings it stirred up. I wonder about my wanting to remain a prisoner rather than return to the game. I wonder about children hurling hard rubber balls at one another with glee. And I wonder about the messages of competition and being chosen that entered our psyches on those rainy days when we couldn't play outside.

I have been thinking about boundaries for several years. Ever since I first heard that there might be such a thing as a personal boundary, I suspected that I was not the only person who would find the concept intriguing. Boundaries protect us and separate us. They hold us in or keep us out. They provide a sense of safety that in an instant can be violated or become quite false.

During the time of researching and writing this book current events in my personal life and in the life of the world convinced me of the need for personal healing. Unless we can heal at the personal level, how can we hope to have an impact globally? Until people can learn to feel safe, they cannot come together as community. Afraid and unprotected by boundaries, people remain separated from one another, in competition, at war. As people learn to recognize and honor the sacredness of their own boundaries and respect those of others, they can begin to honestly share and cooperate. Without increased community and cooperation, personal and global safety are in jeopardy.

CHAPTER 1

The Issue of Boundaries

*T*HIS IS A BOOK ABOUT PERSONAL BOUNDARIES: WHAT they are, how they are established, how they get damaged, how to redefine them, and most of all how to protect them. Without adequate boundaries people are vulnerable and frightened. It is this fear that underlies our compulsive, addictive, and self-destructive urges and behaviors. Like the bombardment players discussed in the Introduction, we are trapped behind enemy lines, giving ourselves up as prisoners; some of us are waiting in vain to be rescued.

Not much has been written specifically about personal boundaries, though it is a crucial concept for healthy human development. Most of us struggle with issues related to boundaries whether we recognize it as that or not. We avoid certain people and places; we unplug our telephones because we are afraid someone

5

will call to ask a favor; we drink too much at parties because it's the only way we can feel comfortable; we spend time with people we don't like because we don't want to hurt their feelings; we never think we look right; someone else always looks better. These are all actions related to personal boundaries. We alter our behavior and shrink our worlds through our futile attempts to feel safe, secure, loved, or accepted. Without well-defined personal boundaries we have very little permission to say what we do and don't want in our lives. We cannot say "No," so we acquiesce, hide, or act out with self-destructive behaviors.

We need personal boundaries for self-protection. When we fail to learn about and incorporate healthy boundaries, we are bombarded by life. Eventually the pain builds, along with a growing awareness that something is wrong. If we manage to continue ignoring our internal distress signals, the pain keeps growing. When the pain gets to be too much, we have to find ways to shut it off. This is where self-destructiveness comes in, commonly in the form of compulsive or addictive behaviors that numb our pain. Establishing personal boundaries requires us to be aware of pain. If we can feel, we can set limits on our experience that don't require us to go completely numb.

While growing up we are indoctrinated into the culture with phrases like "Be polite to others," "Mind your manners," "Don't let the other guy get you down," and "Put on a happy face," all of which send a direct message to deny our instincts, intuition, and feelings for the sake of looking good or coming out ahead. These most certainly are not messages that allow people to assess their inner thoughts and feelings and make decisions that are based on them. More value is placed on looking good and winning than on establishing inner harmony and honest intimacy with other people. We are taught to turn our attention outward, to focus on what other people think of us at the expense of being aware of how we feel inside. We learn that "self-centered" means selfish, an undesirable and bad character trait. "Self-sacrifice" is touted as a virtue. Great rewards are reaped by the most competitive members of society. Winning, making money, and getting ahead all keep our attention focused on beating the other guy. In the process we lose touch with ourselves.

Powerful influences and messages are communicated to us all the time just below the surface of our awareness. When we operate at this level, these messages are not subject to examination and conscious choice. They get taken into our psyches without the benefit of scrutiny and discrimination.

This book attempts to refocus attention and bring a broader set of alternatives into awareness. When we have choices, we can make changes. Without new information we are trapped by earlier decisions. It is time to take a clear look at our boundaries, how they developed or not and what the ramifications are in our current lives.

HUMAN DEVELOPMENT

When a baby is born, he is, to himself, the center of the universe. He is everything. This newborn cannot differentiate between awareness of a situation and the situation itself. He is completely egocentric. By definition this baby is without boundaries.

Human infants are entirely vulnerable at birth. Without adults to provide complete care for an extended period of time, an infant would perish. Babies are equipped with behavioral equipment, specifically their ability to cry, designed to reduce risk and secure the needed adult care. Very strong messages are transmitted to the ego when an infant employs this behavioral equipment. An infant who fails to obtain food and attention through the only means available—crying—will inevitably wind up feeling helpless and distrustful of a world in which his needs cannot be met. An infant whose needs are met consistently and on time will feel secure and safe in the world and will pass through this earliest stage of development without boundary damage.

In the course of human development a child moves from egocentricity toward the ability to see a given situation from another's perspective. He begins to make inferences about other people's experiences. By about age six or seven children can begin to make judgments regarding the expectations of others. For a child whose needs are not consistently met or who has been severely punished, the expectations of other people become the primary focus. This child will constantly be on the lookout for ways to be pleasing or avoid punishment. Conversely, a child who receives consistently responsive care can risk ignoring external expectations and act according to his internal impulses. This child has the safety of an environment that allows for experimenting with self-regulation.

Every human being's sense of identity depends in

large measure on the validation of self by a reference group. The family is the primary reference group for a child. The way the family interacts with itself and with the outside world provides the climate for psychological growth. A family that cannot tolerate the individuality of each of its members demands that children stifle their natural instincts and curiosity for the sake of conforming to the family code. How to express anger is typically one of the earliest lessons a child learns about the family code. Expressing anger is one means of establishing a boundary, of setting a limit. It is an honest statement. If children are punished for these honest outbursts of anger, they learn that it is not safe to express themselves.

In conjunction with the family, a child has ongoing relationships with a variety of other people who provide a steady source of definition of self and other. It is through these interactions and experiences that a child receives the social knowledge of the culture and forms his sense of boundary. As children learn the rules of the society and the culture, they learn the basis for interaction with others. A child learns how to follow a rule before he can understand the concept or make an informed choice. This preverbal learning leaves room for a dangerous gap between "ought" and "is." Children who are drilled into obedience lose contact with their own internal monitoring systems.

Ideally a child is enculturated into relationships that are more or less predictable and safe. A healthy sense of self emerges from one's experiences and the ability to reflect on them. When children fail to learn how to reflect on their experiences, they have difficulty protecting themselves.

For the first eighteen months of life children have no clear idea of who they are; they have no boundaries. An infant depends entirely on his mother and father to provide for his basic needs. It isn't until what we ironically call the "terrible twos" that a child begins to develop some sense of personal boundary. At this time a child begins to push away from his parents and develops the ability to say "No." This is early boundary testing, a time when the child learns what is and what is not within his control. Hopefully this is also the time when a child establishes a unique sense of identity and knows where his stops and another's identity begins.

As children get older, it is through language that they are taught the rules, expectations, and obligations of the culture. Through language children learn how to interpret and evaluate people and events. If children are given answers to their questions and patient explanations, they will continue to explore. When children are silenced or ignored, they will turn away from the world.

As the process of development continues, a child develops skills for self-monitoring and self-correction. These skills may vary, depending on the cultural and family background of the child. Self-monitoring and self-correction skills are the basic building blocks for personal boundaries. The bad news is that many people have deficient or completely nonexistent skills for self-assertion and negotiation. The good news is that boundary skills can be learned.

Simply put, boundaries are our sense of ourselves. They allow us to know who we are, especially as we relate to other people. Boundaries protect us and allow us to be unique. They enable us to get close to other people and permit us to establish distance as well. Without boundaries we would be overwhelmed. Healthy boundaries help us act appropriately toward other people and avoid being abused.

Parents have a tremendous impact on the construction or destruction of boundaries in their children. No parent ever consciously set out with the purpose of destroying his child's boundary system. But many boundaries and many children have been damaged in the name of love and ignorance—damaged by parents who didn't know the importance of allowing their children to explore their own limits, probably because they were never allowed to do so themselves.

PHYSICAL BOUNDARY

Skin is an infant's first means of communication with the outside world. The skin is the largest organ of the body, and it is intricately connected to various message centers in the brain. As a sensory system, skin is by far the most important organ system of the body. Tactile stimulation is a biological requirement for healthy physiological and behavioral development. Therefore, how a baby is held, when, and by whom are all very important initial messages sent to an infant through the only communication channel he perceives, the skin.

The human body very clearly delineates itself. In a sense, our skin is our boundary. Beyond this initial boundary there are spatial boundaries that constitute acceptable and unacceptable levels of closeness. Spatial boundaries are regulated by relationships, individual preference, and the norms of the culture.

Children are taught to distinguish between "public" and "private" in relation to parts of the body, and in a sense this is a lesson about boundaries. Some of the first messages about "public" and "private" probably take place before the child has the capacity for language. The communication takes place through touch: who, how, when, and where others touch the child. How parents respond when their child naturally begins exploring his own body is crucial. For example, parents may be comfortable enough with their own sexuality not to panic when a child discovers his genitalia and learns that touching certain places feels good. But those same parents may not feel so comfortable when the behavior takes place at the grocery story or at Grandma's house. The child gets the message even if no words are spoken.

Forms of address and physical proximity also express intimacy and distance. Some people pass their baby around to anyone who wants to hold him; some are very fearful of having their child out of reach. Both of these styles transmit message about boundaries. The child really has no say in the matter, except perhaps to protest by bursting into tears. Later in life children are taught distinctions about forms of address. Certain adults are addressed formally, while others can be called by first names, sometimes proceeded by the familial role—Aunt, Uncle, etc. Each of these lessons on boundaries shapes the perceptions and conceptions of children; in fact, they shape the framework of the culture.

The most obvious forms of physical boundary violation are physical and sexual abuse. Less obvious forms are neglect and abandonment. In all cases the physical boundary of the child is not respected and nurtured.

When a child receives too much or too little tactile stimulation, inner conflicts emerge that interfere with the child's development. The child is forced to block out both external and internal stimuli, to shut down in order to survive. In other words, the child begins getting numb. In some cases children will lose some of their sensitivity. We may see them as the tough kids, the ones who seem unscathed by anything. In other cases children will withdraw completely, stop talking and interacting, engage in rocking behavior, or slip into severe depression.

Ashley Montagu writes, "I believe that the deprivation of body touch, contact, and movement are the basic causes of a number of emotional disturbances which include depressive and autistic behaviors, hyperactivity, sexual aberration, drug abuse, violence, and aggression."[1]

In an extremely moving book, *No Language but a Cry*, Dr. Richard D'Ambrosio shares the story of a badly scarred, motionless, mute child who had been fried in a pan by her parents when she was eighteen months old. Since that time she had been housed at a state institution staffed by nuns. The child was eight when Dr. D'Ambrosio began working with her, and for several years it seemed unlikely that the child would ever emerge from her withdrawn world. He used play therapy with dolls to draw the girl out. Ultimately, the dolls helped reenact the terrifying events of the child's early trauma. The results were astonishing. This twelve-year-old girl screamed "No, no, no, no." These were the first words she ever uttered.[2]

EMOTIONAL BOUNDARY

Emotional boundaries are formed early in life and are greatly influenced by the nature of the bond with our parents. Healthy emotional boundaries help us honestly determine our feelings about any situation, person, place, or thing. Unhealthy emotional boundaries lead us to dishonesty and overresponsibility toward the feelings of others.

By the second year of life children can make the connection between how they behave and how others will respond. They typically experiment with behavior that is designed to cause distress. This stage of development can be highly stressful for parents and children. Lessons learned about boundaries during this time will influence the rest of the child's life. If children are helped to connect behavior and response with the articulation of feelings, this has a favorable impact on their future behavior. Children whose mothers talk to them about feelings, who explain that certain behaviors cause distress or happiness or sadness, grow up to take their own and other people's feelings into consideration.

Emotional boundaries are damaged when parents do not function as adults and children are forced to become responsible for their parents' needs. These children learn to ignore and deny their own needs. Their emotions become enemies that must be numbed into submission because the children come to believe that feelings are harmful to themselves and those around them.

When parents share adult secrets and worries with a child, they are not respecting the child's emotional boundaries. These children mistakenly take on the problems of adults as if they were their own and become unable to determine their own concerns.

Children who hear repeated messages of blame and humiliation are emotionally abused. The children cower under heavy clouds of guilt and shame that prevent them from setting and maintaining healthy boundaries. These children do not believe they have the right to refuse the desires of others; they feel they don't deserve to set their own limits. Shamed children are so focused on the feelings of others that they are completely out of touch with their own feelings. Shamed children build barriers, not boundaries. They hide behind walls designed to keep other people out. Sadly, these walls keep out healing messages of nurture and compliment as well. People with damaged emotional boundaries cannot say "No."

INTELLECTUAL BOUNDARY

A healthy intellectual boundary allows us to trust our perceptions. It lets us know what we want and what we need as well as what we don't. A healthy intellectual boundary does not confuse our desires with those of other people. A flexible intellectual boundary permits us to accept information from the outside world, scrutinize it, and decide whether to accept it as "ours."

Children need a safe space within which they may

physically and mentally explore. Conflicts and anxieties are worked out by children through play and the use of fantasy long before children can speak and reason. Daydreaming can be a way of resolving confusion and relieving distress. Parents who intrude on or try to manipulate a child's imagination are damaging a most valuable resource.

Parents who control a child's perceptions and vision warp the child's intellectual boundaries and foster dependence and a lack of self-responsibility. Managed children have a hard time trusting their own reality and making healthy decisions that are based on it. As adults, they tend to avoid situations where they need to be decisive or assertive. One woman complained:

> My mother just made up her own version of how it was when I was a kid. It has nothing to do with how it was for me. But when I try to talk to her about what it was like for me, all she can say is "I can't accept that."

Parents who assume they know what a child is thinking and feeling without ever asking and who assign motives to the child's behavior on the basis of these assumptions are violating intellectual boundaries. People with damaged intellectual boundaries forget how to say "No."

SPIRITUAL BOUNDARY

Spirituality is an awareness of our eternal connection to a life force or power of which we are all a part. Spirituality lies beyond religion; it includes all religions. A spiritual boundary allows us to believe there is a power in the universe greater than ourselves. A healthy spiritual boundary lets us embrace our humanness. It allows us to become the persons we were meant to be.

Spiritual abuse takes place when God is used as punishment. Such punishment breeds terror, a combination of shame and fear. Children who hear "God will get you if you don't mind me" or "You will burn in the fires of hell if you ever think of doing that again" develop inaccurate and frightening views of God and a terror that prevents spiritual growth.

Religious guilt is quite possibly the most damaging and extreme form of guilt. There is no escape and no relief. If God is everywhere and is going to get you, where can you go to escape the fear and the guilt? Punishing children with religious guilt separates them from their spirituality, the knowledge of their true source.

Parents who hide behind religious rhetoric, who quote Scripture instead of sharing feelings, breed children for whom a spiritual life is meaningless, empty, and unsatisfying. The words and the rituals are without feeling, and the child is lost. These children may become religious robots like their parents or may reject the teachings altogether and be left with nothing in their place. A man with an overly controlling, critical father describes his reconnecting with a sense of something greater than himself in the universe as follows:

I remember my dad always saying to me as a kid, "Oh, you just think you are holier than thou." It was his way of trying to bring me down a notch or something. I never believed that stuff they taught us at Sunday school, and by the time I had a choice I just stopped going to church at all. So, then, when I got to AA and I was struggling to get some sort of understanding of a higher power, I just couldn't grasp onto anything. My sponsor suggested that I ask for help. I guess what I did was pray. I asked real hard for some help, some clue, something. There he was, my dad, standing with his hands on his hips, just telling me over and over, "You just think you are holier than thou." And then, in a real little voice, I answered him: "No, I don't. I think you are." It was amazing. I knew right then that I had made my father bigger than God, or higher power, or whatever it is that is bigger than all of us. I knew I needed to move him out of the way before I could reconnect with my awareness of something greater than myself. I visualized him as clouds, and I started a wind that just blew him off. A warm and bright light came into my soul. It was a spiritual moment, very healing. I felt connected and safe somehow.

Strict religious beliefs and practices are rigid and exclusive. Those who maintain different beliefs are viewed as outsiders and infidels. Such rigidity and exclusivity run counter to the practice of spirituality that includes all beliefs and remains flexible to the variations of human uniqueness. People with damaged spiritual boundaries are obliterated by "No."

EXERCISE

Sit on the floor and draw a circle around yourself
with chalk. This is your boundary.

Then have a friend push a pillow inside that boundary. The pillow can represent someone with whom you
have conflict or can have a specific identity. (My guess
is that once the exercise is being done, an identity will
emerge for this pillow.)

What happens to your body when this pillow, this
     identity, comes across the boundary that you
     have drawn for yourself?
What happens to your feelings?
What are you going to do about the intrusion?
Are you going to let this pillow stay within your
     boundaries?
Are you going to expel it?
Are you going to take it hostage?

Now imagine that there is another identity, another
pillow, who is working on behalf of the first and *not* in
your best interest.

Imagine that this pillow whispers things like "Oh,
what would _____ say if he knew you were being
so unkind? How can you be so cruel? Don't you know
he was only trying to _____?"

How are you feeling now? Can you recognize the
guilt trip that is being foisted off on you here? Do you
see the vast susceptibility you have to what other people
expect or want? Do you see the price you are paying?

* * *

Is it any wonder that we feel tired and heavy when we carry the weight of everyone else around with us? Take a clear look at where your boundaries are with certain significant people in your life and see whether any territory is under attack.

SAYING "NO" VERSUS MASOCHISM

My fascination with the issue of personal boundaries has been growing for many years. I was in my early twenties, watching the movie *Shoot the Moon*, when a completely new possibility opened up for me, the possibility of saying "No." The daughter in the movie, with whom I heavily identified, an imaginative loner with a blue typewriter, looked right up to her mother during a discussion and said, "I don't want to talk about that right now." A jolt of energy went through my body. I held my breath, waiting for the cinema mom to explode. But there they stood up on the screen with a look between them that might have been love.

"I don't want to talk about that right now." That simple sentence spoke to something deep inside me to which I'd never given voice. I rolled the phrase around in my mind for days, secretly trying it out. "I don't want to talk about that right now." A magical sentence, deliciously powerful, a heady new concept for someone who had never imagined having such a right.

A friend calls to tell me a story. She has been rudely awakened by a not-so-close friend who has come knocking frantically on her door, shouting, "Are you all right, are you all right?" This is a man she has specifically asked to call before ever dropping by. Apparently he has considered a message left on the answering machine two days earlier, which said nothing about a visit, as the fulfillment of this request. So she has been drawn rudely from sleep and is now sitting in her living room face to face with this intruding visitor.

He begins talking about the breakup of his relationship with another woman and his philosophy about what women and men want from sex. My friend is aware of a voice inside herself complaining, "I don't want to be having this conversation with this person." She pulls her robe around herself, tightens her jaw, and lights her third cigarette.

I have talked to many people about this paralysis, this inability to heed the wishes of one's authentic self. Out of fear of doing or saying something that might hurt or disappoint someone else, we sacrifice ourselves. We are killing ourselves in small increments because we can't just say, "No, this isn't a good time for a visit right now" or "I don't think this is an appropriate topic of conversation, and I would like you to stop discussing sexual matters in my presence." Later we know just what we should have said, usually after a few days or hours of mental replay. Then there are those rare times when we know what to say right then. The trouble is, we can also imagine how the other person will feel when he hears what we say, and boom, we silence ourselves. We ignore our feelings in order to spare others'. It is a tactic that leaves people ignored and trivialized. It is a tactic that leaves women abused. Men and women need some permission to express their feelings. Since I think women have more access to feelings and

men have more permission in general, perhaps they can
share in this learning.

Imagining negátive outcomes and responses to our
actions is restricting at best. Over a lifetime it can become paralyzing. I have an internal censor who silences
me with the threat "Oh, she won't want to hear that; it
will just hurt her feelings," and instantly I start trying to
minimize my feelings because I have decided out of
some misplaced sense of courtesy not to share them.
Ultimately I do damage to myself by not honoring my
feelings and needs, and I belittle other people by protecting and monitoring what they can and cannot hear.
The compulsion to inflict suffering on oneself in order
to keep repressed feelings and pain from coming out is
the essence of masochism and self-destructiveness.

By deciding beforehand what someone else should
hear or respond to, we deprive that person of the opportunity for growth and true understanding of himself and
us. Instead of having drawn a boundary for ourselves,
we have constructed a playpen around another person,
treating him like a helpless infant. This is not caring. It
is pure arrogance.

The term *masochism* may bring to mind vicious and
violent acts that most people would say don't apply to
them. But I believe that whenever we silence our emotions, relinquish our power over our destiny, and accept
suffering as our lot in life, we are engaging in behavior
that stems from a masochistic belief system. When we
engage in masochistic behavior, it is not so much that
we take pleasure in pain and suffering, as it is just that
we don't know any other ways to respond. We have no

alternatives, no other resources. Our belief system does not extend beyond the experience of suffering.

Both men and women have experiences early in life that may diminish their resourcefulness and predispose them to a masochistic belief system and behavior patterns. Unfortunately, our culture furthers this reality by continually reinforcing the message to women, "Don't take action. Don't get angry," and to men, "Don't feel your feelings. Don't ever let your vulnerability show."

The problems, illnesses, and syndromes that will be discussed in this book happen to men and to women. But in many cases (particularly anorexia nervosa and agoraphobia) they affect primarily women. In today's atmosphere of greater promise and higher expectations for women, self-destructive or masochistic behavior may be becoming a more common problem. As women find doors opening, they are pulling the rugs out from underneath themselves—starving themselves, locking themselves inside their homes, using drugs, and in the most severe cases killing themselves.

Masochism is a disease that undermines an individual's capacity to stand up for himself, to set and maintain healthy personal boundaries, to say "No." Some examples of masochistic behavior include the following:

Apologizing when someone bumps into you

Apologizing when you drop something, especially if you are alone

Giving lengthy explanations for being five minutes late

Not asking for something until it is too late to get it

Ordering the cheapest item on the menu, especially if you don't like it

Never sending something back with which you are unsatisfied

Overtipping, especially when the service is not superior

Lending other people money

Being unwilling to ask your boss for a raise

Being unable to accept compliments

Being afraid to call someone you don't know on the phone

Compulsively buying, writing, and sending birthday, holiday, thank you, get well, and other greeting cards, always on time

Spending too much time and money on presents you always fear are not "right"

Never thinking you did, sent, or said the "right" thing

Never clearly stating what you want: "I don't know; what do you want to do?"

Having sex to avoid a fight

Having sex to avoid hurting someone else's feelings

Having sex you don't want

Never initiating sex

Not recognizing an unhappy, abusive relationship

Not ending an unhappy, abusive relationship out of fear of being alone

Not ending an unhappy, abusive relationship out of fear of hurting your partner

Believing you are the only one to blame for problems in a relationship

Believing that if you are alone, no one will ever love you again

Anticipating situations in which you will be hurt
Expecting the worst

MAKING IT PERSONAL

Remember the bombardment game I mentioned in the Introduction? I think this game, along with the anxiety I felt whenever we had to play it, has had a formative effect on my fascination with boundaries. The game serves as a metaphor for the vulnerability felt by those with inadequate protection and for the isolation felt by those who have too much.

As players of this game we were all vulnerable to attack from the other side. The only protection we had was the possibly poor throwing skills of the other team's members and our ability to duck from the ball. All of us were on guard all the time until we were taken prisoner. I hated the anticipation and the tension. I hated the aggression and the lack of safety. I always wanted to be taken prisoner in order to avoid feeling threatened and defenseless.

The dictionary defines the verb *disarm* as "to deprive of a means of attack or defense" and "to deprive of a means, reason, or disposition to be hostile." Disarm is what countries can do when they feel that their boundaries are no longer under siege. Personal disarmament is what people can begin doing once they have established boundaries and learned when and how to protect them. Through this disarmament process people can begin to make connections with one another in a more honest and sincere manner. Healthy boundaries facilitate the process of losing the means, reason, and disposition to be hostile.

While trying to find and establish boundaries, I have found it helpful to think of myself as a country. I examine how the country is guarded, whether by kindly police, an armed military, barbed wire fences, or an impenetrable wall. Perhaps there's no protection at all. I look at who is allowed to cross the borders of this country. Who is restricted? Who is denied passage? Who is the enemy? Who is not allowed to cross back out once he has entered? How does communication take place both internally and with the outside world?

As I examined my life and my relationships from this perspective, I discovered an internal disinformation system that feeds me messages that are not always in my best interest. I realized that I had established diplomatic relations that were based on lies. I found that I had denied visas to people who spoke languages that were unfamiliar rather than learning new languages. I saw that I had walled off huge sections of my personal territory with fear. I felt that it was lonely in my country.

The fourth step of the twelve steps of Alcoholics Anonymous states, *"Made a searching and fearless moral inventory of ourselves."* My understanding and practice of this step is to focus inwardly and become aware of my internal situation. It is a turning away from an analysis of the external and a turning toward the internal. Consciousness requires extreme honesty and selfexamination. Becoming aware requires that we shed our assumptions and habits of thought and immerse ourselves in a ruthless examination of our reality. Personal inventory can connect us with the thoughts and feelings that contribute to our anxiety and create our fears. By lessening our personal anxiety we can diminish the supply that we contribute to the anxiety of the world.

Some questions that you might want to consider while examining your internal environment and personal boundaries include the following:

What is your defense system?
Whom do you trust?
Who are your enemies?
What is your relationship to violence?
Do you use weapons as a means of control?
What parts of yourself do you imprison?
Do you torture yourself?
Do you live in a hostile or a benevolent universe?
What do you think is going to cause you harm?
Where are your borders?
Who can cross them?
To whom do you deny entry?
To whom do you deny exit?
What territories are you afraid to enter?
What information do you censor?
Have you been invaded? By whom?
Have you invaded? Whom?
How much territory do you need?

These questions were useful to me while I was trying to generate some concept of my own boundaries. I found that it was easier to look at myself if I took a couple of steps back. You might find that you have to sneak past internal secret police and disinformation channels, but this is all part of achieving consciousness and defining our boundaries. Once you can begin to make "boundary" a distinct concept for yourself, you can begin to make it personal and sacred.

CHAPTER 2

Boundary Invasions

IT IS MY BELIEF THAT MANY SELF-DESTRUCTIVE BEHAViors have their roots in some sort of intrusion on or trauma to personal boundaries during critical periods of development. So what constitutes an intrusion or boundary violation? The most obvious examples are clearly found in physical and sexual abuse. In both cases, physical, mental, and spiritual boundaries are not respected and severe damage is done to the individual. These damages are manifested in a variety of self-destructive behaviors or illnesses.

Physical and sexual abuse are not the only forms of boundary violation. There is a subtle continuum of intrusion that ranges from expectation to comparison and criticism, overprotection, judgmentalism, sexual harassment, and enmeshment to the more overt forms of physical and sexual abuse. Damage to personal boundaries

produce a wide range of adaptive responses, usually
without our conscious awareness. Many of these
responses are self-destructive and not respectful of ourselves. In order to understand and perhaps modify our
responses into greater self-care, it is important to examine how human beings unwittingly intrude upon and
abuse one another.

EXPECTATIONS

I found the following entry in my old journal as I was
putting together the material for this book.

My Own Expectations
Expectations are hope I can't let go of. They are the
hope that I cling to, even if there isn't a chance. The
dimmer the possibility, the tighter I hold. And while
I tighten that grip, I let go of options. I let all of my
choices dry up, shrivel, vanish, all for the sake of
holding on to a dying hope.

Expectations cloud whatever vision of reality I might
ever have had, and they trigger my obsessive thinking and behaving. They are a sticky trap from which
it is hard to get free. A slap-in-the-face dose of reality is needed to break the grasp of expectation.

Others' Expectations
The expectations of other people are a similar jail. A
constriction of impulse, a distortion of the senses,
a performance with only an imaginary audience. A
changing agenda that no one can possibly satisfy. The

expectations of others are rarely stated, but I respond to them like a robot programmed to please. In fact, I have no true idea what it is I am supposed to do to please, anyway. It's a frantic play without stage directions, lights, or an audience. The imagined audience is filled with harsh critics.

Within any expectation lies a wish that gives it life and connects it to our emotions. People do not easily let go of their wishes. Letting go involves the difficult task of realistically assessing alternative possibilities while avoiding looking through the hopeful eyes of a disappointed child.

EXAMPLE

You are at the beach. You've come for a quiet, relaxed day filled with the sound of waves, some sun, and a good book. Someone drives up in a four-wheel-drive vehicle, parks, opens the doors, and turns the radio on full blast. You feel invaded. You react in fury. You confront the driver in anger and wind up getting into a screaming match.

What happened? You went to the beach carrying an expectation for a relaxing day. The expectation is a reasonable one, but the strength with which you hold on to it may be a problem. When this expectation is interrupted, disappointment comes rushing in. It is painful to let go of our wishes, our dreams, and our expectations of how things "should" be. Behind the scenes lurks another hidden expectation that "things like this shouldn't happen to me." This is the expectation that fuels the rage that was your response to the intrusion of a radio into your afternoon. Once this righteous indignation has taken over, alternative thoughts and behaviors become less accessible. Asking the driver to turn down the music, moving, and getting into the water are not available as options once our crushed expectation explodes into a rage.

The self-destructive element here lies in the verbal attack and the accompanying release of adrenaline. A full-blown tirade brings a rush of energy and a grandiose high, both of which can become addictive. The truth is that ranting and raving like that is really only an attempt to bolster our low self-esteem. We puff up like roosters so that no one will see the scrawny, sad little chickens inside. We may get a momentary high, but the radio blares on and we are left with the toxic effects of rage and disappointment. The disease is called rageaholism, and at least in part, it is a disorder concerned with handling disappointment and disillusionment. When we project our disappointments outward onto other people as anger, we are violating their personal boundaries in order to escape our own feelings. And we are damaging ourselves by not honestly feeling our disappointment and sadness.

Then there are people who hold on to their disappointment because without it they fear they will have nothing left. Chronically disappointed individuals do not learn from past experiences. They are rigid and unable to reassess situations on the basis of what is real. They are impaired by a negative belief system that tells them that because things were bad in the past, they will be bad in the future. Perhaps the expectations of these individuals were too high to begin with, but instead of readjusting their expectations in keeping with reality, they remain in a cycle of perpetual disappointment.

I have an expectation that people will do what they say and another that people will be honest. Both of these from time to time cause me great disappointment, frustration, and anger. I am hooked emotionally to both of these ideas, and I take human deviation from my expectation as a personal insult. In those instances my energy is not available for reorganization and movement; it is fixated on my wish and my unwillingness to accept that the wish has not been granted. I get angry. I scream things like "I just can't believe that she told me that everything was going just fine, and she wasn't even working on it at all," or "He was so pleasant and nice about it on the phone, why couldn't he just have said he didn't want to do it in the first place?" My initial tendency is to intrude into the other person's behavior and try to make it different rather than accepting that it is what it is and living within the territory of my disappointment. This is a boundary issue.

At the heart of the problem is an unfulfilled wish I carry from childhood: I should get what I want and deserve not to be disappointed. There is a tenacious little girl inside me who has trouble believing she can survive the feelings that will come if she lets go of this expectation. This is the little girl I wrote about in *Little Miss Perfect*.

Each of us carries wishes, some of which are old and out of date. Some of our wishes refuse to take reality into account and therefore always bring pain. The wishes we carry from childhood have the most strength.

Without our recognizing it, time increases our level of yearning for unmet childhood wishes.

I believe that one cause of compulsive and addictive behaviors is our perpetual denial or lack of acknowledgment of our internal conflict between expectations and reality. Until we can recognize and make peace with what haunts us and hurts us, we are doomed to compulsively eat, clean, socialize, diet, gamble, drink, use drugs, smoke, have sex, cut our wrists—whatever our chosen mode of self-damage may be.

Expectations may draw our attention away from true perception. They color the way we experience reality. We can become so absorbed in our wishes and projections into the future that we can't see what is happening directly in front of us. In this way expectations serve as distractions that limit our experience in the present. When we are totally wrapped up in our expectations, we are anticipating the future rather than experiencing the adventure of life as it unfolds in the present.

Far from being entirely negative, expectations serve a very useful purpose. Without expectations we could not make plans for the future, prepare for things, or believe that the future will actually happen. Expectations also provide a sense of security that keeps us from being overwhelmed by unexpected events. Expectations are connected to our imagination and affect both how we behave in the world and, conversely, how the world behaves toward us. Our past experiences affect what we are able to imagine but need not dictate or limit our present and future possibilities.

On September 22, 1989, less than one year after I moved to the beach, a severe hurricane smashed the coastline of South Carolina and rearranged many years' worth of expectation and pleasant imagining I had had about what living on a beach would be like. On the days leading up to landfall I was hopeful. In fact, until the very last moment I was unrealistically optimistic that the storm would veer off and spare us entirely. My imagination simply would not permit devastation to become the picture it could see.

After the storm, my house was still standing but there was tremendous chaos and destruction everywhere. The dream I had carried for years of an idyllic, tranquil life on a beach had been shattered, yet I remained desperate to hold on to it. I clung to wishes that things would quickly get better while I painfully absorbed the reality of all that had been lost. I shifted into high gear with cleaning up, trying unsuccessfully to put everything back as it had been. It was many months before I was able to mourn, bury my dream, and accept the true reality of the full range of possibilities that comes with living on a coast.

We have become a society that believes in the promise of the quick fix. We have fast food, pop psychology, microwave ovens, bank teller machines, automatic everything. We watch television, where all conflicts can be resolved in a thirty- or sixty-minute time period with commercial interruptions. We are addicted to the promise of instant, guaranteed satisfaction. We're afraid of disappointment; we do not see it as an opportunity to regain flexibility and ingenuity.

The media and advertising are constantly bombarding us with images and wishes. They define how we should look, what we should wear, what size we should be, and even the eye color we should have. Since very few of us can attain even a small part of these projected images, we all walk around feeling inadequate.

We carry the images and suggestions provided by the media. Yet they are an intrusion; they soil our minds. They are an interruption of our well-being, an invasion of our state of mind. And worst of all, they are a lie.

FAMILY EXPECTATIONS

It is proper, even desirable, for parents to have expectations that their children will be honest, polite, intelligent, respectful, and self-directed. But sometimes parents hold expectations that surpass a child's developmental level. Problems arise in a family where a child doesn't have the qualities that make him what the parents need and expect. Such parental expectations can frustrate and devour a child's developing self. Parents who try to raise children in their own image manage only to raise children who fail to develop a personality of their own and experience life by living it through someone else.

Children who fear losing love and nurturance as a result of disappointing parental expectations are forced to bury their true feelings and murder a part of themselves. Boundaries are invaded by parents who cannot accept their children's individual choices and directions. Little girls are shamed for wanting to play with Legos instead of Barbie. A teenage boy is belittled for wanting to study landscaping instead of business. Socialite parents criticize a daughter who is quiet and shy. A college graduate is given a gift of a suit and tie instead of the

equipment he needs for an upcoming white-water raft-
ing trip. As I said, it is generally appropriate for parents
to have hopes and dreams for their children. When
those hopes and dreams are so rigid that they no longer
allow for the individuality of children, they are boundary violations.

In the first few moments after birth, messages are
passed from the parent to the infant concerning appearance, sex, and approval or disapproval of various expectations. These messages are passed through touch, the
only type of communication a newborn can understand.
Before a child has speech he has to rely on whatever
sources of communication are available. Touch is a major source, but so are intuition and unconscious communication. A child is strongly influenced by the
unconscious mind of his parents. If a child is perceived
by one or both parents as a disappointment, the message
goes directly to the child. For parents who are unhappy
with some aspect of the new baby, the reality of crying
and diaper soiling and other perfectly normal infant behaviors can be viewed as negative and the critical bond
of love does not develop and strengthen.

Children need physical care and protection, nurturance, love, the opportunity to relate to others, and help
in relating to the world by organizing and mastering
their experience. They need these things from their parents. Parents are expected to recognize and meet these
needs, often with no more reward than just knowing
that they are doing so. There may be conflict when the
child's need and the parents' need collide. Ideally it is
up to the parents to meet their own needs without interfering with those of the child. This is a difficult thing

for many parents to do, especially parents whose own childhood needs went unmet. It is a cycle that leads to abuse.

Parents who silence their children, rearrange their memories, never let them express their opinions, and push them beyond the limits of their competency raise children who are easily intimidated, have chronically low self-esteem, meet the needs of other people at a high cost to themselves, and find it almost impossible to satisfy their own needs. Passivity is an insidious form of self-destructiveness fostered by a lack of self-confidence.

Families have codes about what is allowed and what is not. There are rules of communication: who talks to whom, when, and how. There are rules about the demonstration of feelings: which are acceptable and which are not. And there are rules of conduct: how everyone behaves within the family as well as how each individual is to act outside the family. The rules are not necessarily stated outright, but each family member knows what they are. It is these unspoken rules that generally protect the family secrets and keep the family looking good to the outside world. Some of the family rules that stunt children's healthy development include the following:

Don't talk back
Always be polite
Don't be angry
Don't be sad
Always be good
Think as we do

Don't grow up

You've got to do it right the first time

Always look good because appearances are everything

Do what I say, not what I do

Don't be selfish

Don't talk outside the home about what goes on inside

Mind your manners, no matter how you feel

Children who must decipher and obey strict family codes quickly lose touch with their internal world and become guardians of the family image. These children lose the ability to explore and learn. They cannot learn from their experiences and fail to learn how to set limits for themselves. This is spiritual and intellectual boundary violation.

Along with strict codes of behavior, families have secrets. Family secrets fall under the category of disinformation systems. They are the things that everyone must pretend are not true or didn't really happen. They are the lies that pass from generation to generation. Expecting children to behave in ways that protect the secrets of adults is a violation of the boundary within which it is safe to be a child. Parents may even go so far as to rearrange memories by telling children that what they experienced really wasn't what happened. This is one way in which family secrets are protected and children are abused. I have talked to many people who are unsure about the events of their childhoods. John told me,

I remember one thing, and my dad remembers another. Somehow, even though it happened to me, my father's memory is the one that sticks. It's almost like everyone is trying to be convinced that the truth didn't happen.

Family secrets include things such as financial problems, mental retardation, lost employment, unexplained death or disappearance, extramarital affairs, mental illness, alcoholism, drug addiction, physical or sexual abuse, and incest. The list goes on and on. Family secrets can also involve a private shame within the family that would not necessarily be seen as a problem by anyone on the outside.

ENMESHMENT

Every family is a system, each member of which plays a part in how the system works. Within the larger system there are subsystems. The spousal subsystem has a boundary that does not include children, for example. The boundaries around these subsystems define how family members interact with one another.

Families operate and interact in a variety of ways, one of which is described as *enmeshment*. In an enmeshed family individual boundaries are poorly defined, weak, and easily crossed. There is generally a lack of physical or emotional privacy within these families. Any type of personal boundary is generally not recognized or respected. The family operates as a single unit, and individuals are simply part of the whole. Family members typically intrude on each other's thoughts and feelings. The boundaries that define individual autonomy are so weak that individuality is virtually obliterated.

Some parents invade their children's privacy to the extent that they try to control the children's fantasy lives. Such parents interrupt their children's normal, healthy dealing with personal issues and conflict through the use of fantasy. They send messages like "Stop daydreaming," "You don't really think that, do you?" and "You're just too young to know any better." Intrusion on a child's process of coping and understanding is very damaging. A child has the right to a private fantasy life, and when parents interfere, they are abusing their children. Such children will grow into adults who censor and silence their intuition and imagination. They will be cut off from their true sources of knowledge.

Intrusive parents have little respect for their children's privacy. This privacy includes possessions, secrets, letters, feelings, and even bodies. This lack of respect for a child's privacy is a symptom of the parents' desire to possess the child. Parents who have unhealthy boundaries are capable of sexually abusing children and believing that a child actually wants this type of interaction. These parents truly believe that they know what is "best" and will unmercifully beat home their point. Intrusive parents rearrange a child's perception, leaving him wondering if he can trust himself. These boundary invasions are severely damaging.

Enmeshed families tend to speak for one another, to finish each other's sentences. There are uneven speaking patterns within the system. For instance, the father talks to the mother through the daughter or all the members pass messages back and forth through one another.

EXAMPLE

Brenda calls her sister to find out if their mother liked the present Brenda sent.

Calling another family member to get information about a third party is the classic triangulated communication model of the enmeshed family system. Individuals cannot speak directly and honestly to one another, so a system that bypasses direct communication develops. Enmeshed families typically communicate feelings as well as facts in this third-party way. Such emotional scapegoating typically sets up children for abuse. If Mom takes out her anger at Dad on the children, they are being abused. When Dad acts out his frustration sexually with the daughter, abuse is taking place. A family that cannot directly communicate feelings fails to produce children who are emotionally healthy and in possession of healthy boundaries.

Babies are born completely without boundaries. It is through interactions with parents and/or primary caretakers that valuable information about safety and vulnerability is transmitted. These are the early building blocks for the establishment of personal boundaries. If a child's early experiences send a message that the world is not a safe and nurturing place, subsequent boundaries will reflect this.

Throughout our lifetime personal boundaries need to be reexamined and adjusted as conditions in life change. You are the only expert on your boundaries. If someone else is trying to tell you where your boundaries are or urging you to change them, your boundaries are being violated. Failure to establish and maintain healthy boundaries results in a perpetual sense of threat, an uncertain sense of personal safety and well-being that in turn produces defense mechanisms. These defense mechanisms help us ignore the self-destructive and abusive elements in our lives.

It is vital that our boundaries be of our own choosing and construction rather than exist at the urgent suggestion of someone else. Otherwise we will be continually violated and not know how to prevent it. If you grew up enmeshed within your family, with an unclear picture of yourself as an autonomous individual, you need to reconsider your boundaries.

OVERPROTECTION

Children need certain things from parents: support, love, encouragement, and stability. They need healthy role models. All children need to be accepted as unique individuals. A respect for the uniqueness of human beings is a basic building block for fundamental well-being.

Parents need to be flexible about a child's self-directed needs. This is one of the most enormous challenges of parenting. Parents should consider that a child often knows what he needs. Those who cannot respect this wisdom prevent their children from knowing themselves and learning what is right for them. Parents who cannot respect a child's self-direction teach only obedience; they do not contribute to curiosity, imagination, and creativity. Rigid parents prevent normal, healthy separation from their children and damage the development of healthy spirituality. Children must be given the chance to experience the consequences of their actions within age-appropriate limits. Children learn by exploring, creating, and making mistakes. Parents who cannot tolerate their children's mistakes or who may blindly punish them or take over responsibility for the errors are emotionally abusive.

Some parents adopt a hands-off attitude and fail to provide the limits, structure, and discipline a child needs. These children may feel abandoned by their parents and typically act this out by continually doing "bad" things in an attempt to make the parent set some limits.

Other parents go well beyond healthy bonding, into bondage. This approach does not allow the child to develop independence. Overprotection deprives children of the experience of finding the tools they will need to survive safely in the real world. It keeps them from learning how to protect themselves.

EXAMPLE

Marsha doesn't think her teenage daughter is old enough to take a trip with her classmates to Washington, D.C. The daughter desperately wants to go, but her mother refuses. The daughter accuses her mother of not trusting her. Marsha tells her daughter she is naive and doesn't know all the possible dangers in the world.

This example is tricky because there is a legitimate argument that parents need to protect their children in an increasingly unsafe world. But in this case the mother is preventing her daughter from participating in age-appropriate behavior—an outing with peers—because of her own fears, masked as concern for the child. Experience is an excellent teacher; it breeds knowledge. Overprotection, on the other hand, breeds only a high degree of fearfulness or outright defiance.

Parents who constantly anticipate catastrophes send loud messages that they don't trust a child's ability to get along in the world. They also interfere with a child's experience of the world by filling the child's mind with fear. Marsha's mother believes that she is being loving and caring, but her daughter gets the message that she is weak, helpless, and not to be trusted with the challenges of life. Here, too, is an example of spiritual boundary violation. The mother is unable to exercise flexibility and allow for the self-directed needs of her child. She is unable to support her daughter's dreams.

CRITICISM AND COMPARISON

Criticism, when it is used constructively and not to diminish or shame another person, can be a useful source of observation and insight. Comparison, by contrast, when used for anything other than shopping, is abusive.

When we look in magazines and compare ourselves with the slick men and women there, we are abusing ourselves. When a friend responds to our emotional outburst by saying, "Jane would never get so worked up over something so simple; why are you?" we are being abused. When we ask a partner to act or be more like someone else, we are abusing that person. When we use comparison to boost our self-esteem, we are abusing ourselves and others.

EXAMPLE

When waiting in grocery checkout lines, I have a bad habit of mentally sizing up people on the basis of what sorts of food they have in their carts.

Maybe I had a hard day, a disappointment, or a fight with a friend. Perhaps I'm not liking myself today because I'm too fat, too lazy, and unable to play concert piano or should have known the cat was sick before the vet closed for the day. The possibilities are endless.

So here I am, feeling a little down about myself in the checkout line. Instead of reading the tabloids or thumbing through *TV Guide*, I am engaging in idle yet deliberate critical judgmentalism. I have left my body standing in line while my mind intrudes into the private lives and eating habits of complete strangers. Sometimes, when I'm really hating myself, I go even further: I start making critical assumptions about the character and home life of a person from the food in the cart. My assessments are almost never favorable. I am harsh and unforgiving in my judgments. No one in the checkout line has any idea of my mental machinations. I am the only person being harmed by the activity. In my judgmentalism I am violating boundaries, my own and others'.

This may seem like a ridiculous example, but we all criticize and compare ourselves with strangers all the time, even if we don't recognize that we are doing so. Comparison is an unhealthy and unloving practice stemming from feelings about ourselves that are so lousy that we create competitions with complete strangers so that we can come out ahead. We raise ourselves up by putting others down. Ultimately the practice is self-destructive.

When we criticize other people—"She is such a snob" or "He is really a lazy idiot"—we are shifting attention off ourselves and onto others in a critical manner. Shifting our attention outward and projecting judgments onto others are intrusive. Facts are observable actions. Judgments are our conclusions about those actions. Whenever we talk about other people, unless we are describing their actions, we are evaluating them and thereby violating personal boundaries.

It is important to make the semantic distinction between *judgment* and *judgmental*. In the process of trying to shed the harsh behavior of being judgmental, some of us make the mistake of throwing out all judgment whatsoever. This is a boundary violation that leaves us defenseless. Judgment allows us to assess people and situations so that we can decide how to proceed. Judgment allows us to honor and protect our boundaries. Judgmentalism adds a condemning layer to judgment, allowing us to falsely feel superior while violating another's boundaries.

EXAMPLE

In the example of the grocery store, if I were able to confine my thoughts to "I don't care for that soda pop," I would merely be exercising my judgment. But when I venture over into "It's really true; you are what you eat. Look at how bad that guy looks. He ought to eat better," I have crossed over into judgmentalism.

Judging people, situations, or events can be protective. Preemptively judging people, situations, or events can be destructive. If you sum up another person before meeting him or an experience before having it, you isolate and insulate yourself from the world around you. Whenever we put ourselves in the position of judging what is "best" for others, putting our judgment ahead of theirs, we are damaging their boundaries.

Children learn about boundaries from how they are treated and by watching how people treat one another. Parents who were unable to establish and maintain adequate boundaries in their process of development have a hard time accepting the boundaries of their children. I suspect that all parents do the very best parenting they can, yet certain styles of parenting can cause problems.

Positive parents help children find the energy and resources necessary to achieve their goals. Parents who are overly critical of their children produce hypersensitive and insecure personalities. Children know where they are lacking and do not need to be continually reminded. An overly critical parent can quickly destroy a child's motivation by filling the child with shame. These children believe they are bad and unlovable. This is spiritual and emotional boundary damage.

Intrusive parents cannot tolerate their children's separate personalities. These parents offer a distorted sense of reality to the child by seeing everything from only one perspective, their own. Examples of critical responses that devalue the child's uniqueness include statements like "How could you do this to me?" "What on earth makes you think you're so special?" "When you grow up, you won't be so stupid," and "You went out of your way just to spite me." These statements call for justification and explanation rather than allowing children to be children without shame. It is impossible for children to understand that opinions, especially those of their parents, are not facts and that criticism is only opinion.

I grew up under a sentence that read, "You are so selfish; you think you are so superior." I heard it to the exclusion of "You are smart, or pretty, or loved." I came to fear this indictment of "selfishness" and worked feverishly to erase my self. I became the invisible child, undefined, the one who would draw herself with the invisible crayon. But inwardly I was desperate for role models. I was looking for them everywhere. I read biography, autobiography, and history, looking for a life to copy. I watched people around me, imitating characteristics I liked. I swung madly to the other extreme and became self-less. In everything I did I tried to be pleasing and helpful to others. Finally, the emotional and financial cost of trying to prove that I was not selfish became so great that I had to make an honest reassessment of the facts. I had to banish the messages from the past and replace them with the truth. I had to learn to practice healthy selfishness, to put the protective boundary back in place. My first book, *Little Miss Perfect*, is the chronicle of that journey.

PUNISHMENT

The disciplining of children is one area where people greatly disagree about what constitutes appropriate punishment and what crosses over into child abuse. In addition, child-rearing practices are generally protected from outside scrutiny by the sacrosanctity of the nuclear family. Where is the line drawn between harmless "spanking" and the actual beating of a child? What is the difference between setting a limit and posing a threat? How can we expect parents to raise and discipline children in ways different from the way they were raised? And if there was abuse in their background, how can we expect that it will not be passed on to the next generation? One of the problems is that people deny or minimize childhood abuse. "It wasn't so bad." "Yeah, my dad would beat us when he was mad, but I turned out all right." Or they rearrange the details to avoid facing the pain.

Children need to idealize their parents and believe that they themselves are loved. They will go to great lengths to create explanations and excuses to preserve the belief that their parents are fine and loving. The needlessly stressful punishments to which some parents subject their children lead to the establishment of all sorts of fears in children. They fear that they will be abandoned, slapped, or ignored. They become filled with shame. Children will repress memories and deaden their feelings in order to protect parents who are abusive. This constitutes an early introduction to self-destructive behavior, the squashing of the self to protect another.

As a culture we hold a value that states that children should strive to forgive their parents. After all, parents are doing the best they can. Society at large supports this same idea: parents should be forgiven. This goal encourages children to repress their feelings and feel guilty. The truth of the matter is that sometimes parents do horrible things to children. The price of this forgiveness is that children are forced to forget. True forgiveness is not really possible until children have the reasoning powers that come with maturity. To force forgiveness is to violate a developmental boundary.

Children are defenseless, completely at the mercy of adults. As such, they need to be protected, and their needs must be attended to, not thwarted and punished to meet the parents' sensibilities and schedules. But instead of protecting children our culture provides messages that protect parents. Ideas like "Spare the rod and spoil the child," "Parents know best," "Children are unmanageable," and "Parents must be respected at all times" all contribute to a consciousness that puts children at risk. Children who are not protected will not learn how to protect themselves. Their boundaries will be weak and undefined.

SEXUAL HARASSMENT

I am disturbed by how many people, particularly women, do not feel entitled to use the word *no*. In our culture "No" has come to mean "I don't like you" or "That's a stupid idea" instead of representing a personal statement of unacceptability or noncompliance. "No" has lost its ability to establish limits and boundaries around the user. In a futile attempt to avoid being displeasing or contrary we have forfeited a means of protecting ourselves. This loss contributes to our self-destructiveness.

It would seem that the boundaries between personal

and private, professional and public, have all blurred together, leaving us vulnerable and feeling a high degree
of confusion. The executive secretary who feels unable
to turn down an invitation for drinks after work because
of the ramifications it might present for continued employment is being held hostage by these blurred boundaries. The neighbor who shares with other neighbors the
intimate medical details of a friend's illness without that
friend's consent is not honoring the boundary of privacy. The husband who talks about his marital problems
with anyone who'll listen is crossing the boundary between personal and public. There are countless examples of how boundaries get shaded, blurred, crossed,
and violated. Until we begin to make distinctions about
our boundaries, we cannot hope to protect them.

Without the use of "No," men and women are forced
to do things they don't want to do, be treated in ways
they don't like, and fulfill the wishes and expectations
of everyone but themselves.

Women, in particular, who are traditionally raised to
be sensitive and not to offend, are keenly susceptible to
measuring their self-worth by the positive regard they
receive from others. Such women are so vulnerable and
submissive that they are in danger.

A friend shared a story with me recently. He told of
being on a hike with a group of people who didn't all
know one another. One of the men on this hike spent a
great deal of time talking to one of the women. My
friend described the interaction as "badgering." The
man was telling her his life story and trying to get her
to pay attention to him. She was resisting his efforts
and, according to my friend, appeared completely unin-

terested in this man. At the end of the day the man still had not gotten the message and asked the woman for her telephone number. She gave it to him.

My friend asked her later, "Why did you do that? Why did you give him your number?"

She answered, "I'll just put the answering machine on and not answer the phone."

Now, here is a woman who will alter her behavior and screen her telephone calls rather than honestly state her disinterest in a date. Perhaps she is sparing his feelings, but is anything really being spared by her lie?

It is remarkable and sad how many females do not feel entitled to use the word *no*. It is as if the word verged on profanity. Our culture has perpetrated and accentuated restrictions on personal autonomy with comments like "She really means yes when she says no." Others insinuate that women participate in rape by wearing certain clothing or being in certain places at the "wrong" time. Even when women do say "No," it is not given the value it deserves.

Men, too, may be held captive by the idea that "No" is always a rejection to be avoided. I do not intend to indicate that only women are violated by the cultural conspiracy that dictates that we be polite and meet the expectations of everyone but ourselves. It just appears to me that women are affected more frequently and more violently.

Sexual harassment is a major issue in our society. It appears as yet another manifestation of the biggest boundary invasion of them all: the idea that women are possessions. This mentality teaches women that their self-liking can come only from others in return for their pleasing services and attitudes. The result is vulnerable, passive, and acquiescent women with no power who feel trapped and angry. Women have been taken hostage within their own culture.

TOXIC TRESPASS

We can no longer live in childish egocentricity, without regard for the other beings around us. Earth is becoming a stricter mother. Just as every child needs to have some limits set in order to learn how to live in the world with respect for others, Earth is now making clear to us what her personal boundaries are, and she is insisting that we respect them.[1]

Shakti Gawain, *Return to the Garden*

Pollution comes in many forms, and all of it invades the physical boundary of health and well-being. For some people, noise is as irritating as acid rain. For others, garbage along the side of the riverbank is as distressing as an oil spill on pristine waters. In each case our senses, our sensibilities, and even our bodies and souls are being assaulted.

Court cases are currently being fought in which plaintiffs are asking for damages based on the stress and injury caused by the toxic emissions of industry. The premise states that emotional and physical trespass merits reparation.

In the world today we are so fixated on living comfortably and conveniently that we have jeopardized what may turn out to be our only true protection, the

ozone layer of the earth. In this we may have partici-
pated in the ultimate self-destructive act.

While damage to personal boundaries may result in
individual self-destructive behaviors, damage to plane-
tary boundaries is most certain to be the last straw. It is
my hope that if we can work on the personal level to
build and maintain healthy boundaries, if we can draw
together as a world community instead of being isolated
individuals, we will lessen the dangers the planet currently faces.

I'm taken back to that rainy day on the basketball
court, playing bombardment, caught behind enemy
lines, waiting for a fellow teammate to sacrifice the
glory of taking her own hostage and throw the ball to
me so that I can get free. It is in this act of forfeiting
our personal and immediate gratifications that we begin
to heal. When we no longer feel so deprived that we
must grasp for everything we can acquire, we will be
coming back to center within our own boundaries.

Our healthy, true center of consciousness is damaged
when we're filled with greed and envy, worrying about
what someone else has and how to get it. This is when
people are capable of committing atrocities, when their
consciousness exists on the outside and they become
vacant shells. When people believe they have absolute
power over the earth, when they believe they can control the environment, they believe that everything they
do will be all right. These people actually believe that if
they pollute the oceans and fish and those same fish are
eaten by humans, there will be no problem. When
enough people ignore the planet's boundaries, we are all
in grave danger. Unfortunately, this is the state of affairs

at present, but the present can be transformed as it becomes the future.

EXAMPLE

In your community there is a warning against eating fish caught in the river because an industry is pumping toxins into it upstream. Industry's response is that to change the production methods would be too costly, and it argues that the risk from the toxic discharge has not been conclusively proved.

Obviously, if there is a risk of being poisoned by eating food, our bodies are being put at risk. Physical boundaries have been crossed without our consent. Cloaked in greedy profit margins, industry hides behind its justifications and extends itself outward, causing damage to the planet. This is a destructive policy, and we all suffer.

I think damaged boundaries and an uncentered sense of ourselves permit atrocities like the poisoning of water and air. The collective powerlessness fostered by a culture that has robbed us of "No" has created an evil brew.

A few years ago there was a environmental special on television that ended with a star-studded crowd of people shouting "No" in a collective effort to stop the destruction and the pollution. I remember watching with tears streaming down my face, hugging myself, and saying softly, "Yes, oh, yes, *no* is the answer."

People engage in a wide range of self-destructiveness, from the seemingly harmless to the outrageously harmful. The following sections represent some of the more serious self-destructive or self-limiting behaviors and adaptations people develop. I have chosen to interpret them through the lens of boundary violation. I recognize that some people would argue that there are biochemical reasons for these diseases as well. I am not suggesting that damaged boundaries are the singular contributing factor. I only wish to suggest another angle from which to view human motivation and behavior.

EATING DISORDERS

Anorexia nervosa is one of the most serious psychiatric disorders facing young people. It has the distinction of being one of the few psychiatric illnesses that may produce death. It is a disease primarily affecting young women of privilege. Less than 10 percent of the more than 300,000 cases in the United States involve young men, and rarely are the poor afflicted by this disease. Tens of thousands of young, rich, beautiful women starve themselves into devastating weight loss. Why?

Anorexic women describe their lives as an ordeal of wanting to live up to the expectations of others while always fearing that they are not good enough. They believe they are disappointing failures. They feel unworthy of their position and privilege. Many are overwhelmed by the vast number of opportunities before them, unsure of what they "ought" to do. They are afraid of not choosing correctly. Their attention is riveted outside their own desires. These young women turn to the function of eating in an effort to solve problems in other areas of their lives. They engage in a relentless competition with food that constitutes an ongoing passive suicide.

To lose weight becomes the only success these young women feel they can attain. Their unsuccessful attempts to control their lives are defiantly acted out by their bodies through the control of food intake. Children who are unable to live up to the excessively high expectations of their parents frequently become depressed and unmotivated. Anorexia nervosa is another classic reaction. In this case, however, there is strict motivation and focus.

Anorexia suggests to me an exaggerated attempt to establish a boundary between outside expectations and an unformed internal desire to "be" something. In the absence of a set goal, these young women can turn to a well-publicized goal for all women: "to be thin."

The disease itself is full of contradictions and paradoxes that reflect the internal confusion of the young women who manifest it. While being bombarded from the outside with options, privilege, and expectations, whether stated or not, these women are being attacked from within by feelings of unworthiness, powerlessness, and guilt. They feel "out of control," so they take rigid control over their eating habits. They lose weight and get dangerously thin, yet they do not see themselves as thin. Rather, they see themselves as fat and claim they do not feel hunger. For many of these women their bodies become "the enemy" with which they fight. Unable to find other sources of good feeling, they turn to self-abuse for a sense of accomplishment and success. This is a physical boundary violation and most certainly is self-destructive.

Women suffering from anorexia nervosa typically come from a background where their needs appear to be met when in fact they are not. Within the anorectic family, possessions and maintaining appearances are valued above individuality and self-love. From the outside it looks like a congenial family, but behind closed doors the family is suffocating from so much enmeshment that the child cannot separate and develop her own individuality. The child becomes excessively conforming and in the process ceases to develop. Anorexia is a visible metaphor for this developmental balking. Young girls with anorexia successfully impair their physical development by depriving themselves of adequate nutrition.

There is much preoccupation with the way things look in families that spawn anorexics. What it will look like and what other people will think are valued over and above the feelings of individual family members. There is an image, a perfect veneer, that must be maintained. A complete lack of personal boundaries can be seen in the anorexic's lack of self-esteem and substitute preoccupation with realizing the image she believes others project on her.

Polite behavior is typically emphasized in the families of anorexics. The expression of anger is generally not allowed. Nonexpression of feelings, particularly "negative" ones, is the rule. This is the familial "gag order" that contributes to anorexic behavior.

A spiritual boundary violation characteristic of the anorexic family system is that the young woman is not seen or acknowledged as an individual in her own right. Instead, she is seen as a commodity, someone or even something that can enhance the experience, prestige, and appearance of the family. Left without a voice, the anorexic is screaming through her actions for the formation of a personal boundary so that she can become physically real to those around her. Typically parents are unaware that they have exercised excessive control over an anorexic child. They do not see how they have violated her intellectual and spiritual boundaries by reshaping her reality, correcting her thoughts, and defining her. By refusing to eat, an anorexic is desperately trying to maintain a physical boundary.

Anorexic patients describe not being able to define what they "want" apart from what their parents expect of them. They have been robbed of their sense of self to that degree. Consequently, expressions of self-hatred and self-punishment become crystallized around issues of eating.

A young woman who develops anorexia has a self-concept that she cannot differentiate from her parents'. This is the ultimate in family enmeshment. She may be left feeling that it is unsafe to grow up and separate because, to her, the parents are actually she. She has no boundary of her own within which to develop. Anorexia does have the consequence of arresting physical development while also providing a primary relationship that will not take a young woman far from home. Teenagers suffering from eating disorders have been shown consistently to distort their body size and weight. They have extremely negative and self-denigrating feelings about their personal attractiveness and are uncomfortable with the normal development associated with puberty.

It is a curious paradox that these young women, who receive so many of what our culture considers privileges, wind up feeling a tremendous burden. An anorexic girl, unable to accept the privilege or abundance that has been provided by her fortunate birth, unable to accept herself as a unique individual, turns to self-punishment. She shames and mutilates herself rather than reveling in the gifts she has received. For most, the idea that they have the right to ask for something just for themselves has never occurred. They are more accustomed to guessing what other people want and doing whatever is needed to provide it.

Anorexics, like most women in our culture, are trained to be highly competitive with other women. They keep a constant running mental tabulation of how other women compare. They use other women as a catalyst for self-hatred and criticism. In a desperate attempt to bolster self-esteem, anorexics take pleasure in the fact that they are thinner, even when their thinness looks like starvation.

The flip side of the eating disorder coin is, of course, overeating and obesity. Both are evidenced by huge segments of the population, male and female. Both anorexia and compulsive eating are self-destructive attempts to protect oneself and modulate one's feelings. People do not overeat because they are physiologically hungry, but because they are emotionally starving. The pain we carry from childhood has left us with a hurt child inside. This hurt child is struggling for some recognition and resolution without realizing the damage being done in the process.

Some women and men who suffer from eating disorders are also sexual abuse and incest survivors. Food becomes a substitute for other things that are missing in one's life, such as friends, sexuality, love, recognition, and power. Eating is on some level gratifying, so under stress the behavior is continued. Perhaps being large lessens the feelings of vulnerability that result from the severe boundary damage caused by sexual abuse. Learning to say "No" is the way to regain the power that was taken from us as children. When we can say "No" to people, behavior, and situations that violate our boundaries, we can begin to say "No" to our self-destructiveness.

The behavior of eating large amounts of food defies the boundary of a full stomach. But the issue here is not so much hunger as it is emotional pain turned to self-destructive behavior. In her book *The Obsession*, Kim Chernin describes the behavior as follows:

> I feel that I am about to remember something and then, unaccountably, I am moved to tears. But I do not cry, I say nothing, I look furtively around me, hoping this wave of strong feeling has not been observed. And then, I am eating. My hand is reaching out. And the movement, even in the first moments, seems driven and compulsive. I am not hungry. I had pushed my plate away moments before. But my hand is reaching and I know that I am reaching for something that has been lost. I hope for much from the food that is on the table before me but suddenly it seems to me that nothing will ever still this hunger—an immense implacable craving that I do not remember having felt before.[2]

In contrast to anorexia nervosa, overeating generally affects the poorer, nonprivileged segments of society. It appears that for compulsive eaters the act of eating becomes a way of literally setting a physical boundary around oneself, a large, thick buffer against emotional pain. Not surprisingly, since eating habits and styles of coping with feelings are typically learned within the home, we generally find more than one obese person in a family.

We have examined the boundary violations of excessive family expectation and comparison as they operate in the destruction of boundaries and the instigation of self-destructive behavior. Before leaving the topic of eating disorders I think it's important to explore a possible male counterpart, excessive exercising, or as one friend of mine calls it, gymaholism.

We have become a nation of exercise fanatics. We have begun to use exercise as more than a way to have fun and be healthy. We have turned it into an addiction, a quick fix, a drug. We do it, we talk about it, we intend to do it, and we feel guilty when we don't. In general, we obsess about it.

Exercise, even though it is good for us, takes on abusive characteristics when it becomes a person's primary avenue to self-acceptance, a substitute for people and fun in one's life. When exercise is a way to pump up a false sense of self-esteem rather than pumping up muscle, it becomes a self-limiting addiction.

It is not hard to make the leap into thinking that many of the same forces that propel young women into eating disorders and a preoccupation with their bodies also operate to lead young men into excessive bodybuilding and the use of steroids.

AGORAPHOBIA

In their book *Women Who Marry Houses*, Robert Seidenberg and Karen DeCrow state than an estimated five million to twenty million individuals suffer from agoraphobia in the United States. Eighty-eight percent of these people are women, and most of them are married.[3] Agoraphobia is described as an incapacitating anxiety caused by traveling away from the presumed safety of home. One of the first symptoms of agoraphobia is the inability to shop.

Women who develop agoraphobia generally come from families where childlike interests were not tolerated. They were forced to grow up in a hurry, to become self-reliant and independent. As children they cloak themselves in behaviors and qualities that give them the illusion of strength and self-sufficiency. In adulthood the facade begins to crumble.

Technically, a woman suffering from agoraphobia has returned to the childlike, dependent state she missed as a child. She places herself in the demeaning and precarious position of being dependent on the generosity of another. Like the parent, the caregiver can exercise the power to withdraw or to demand.

There is another way to view agoraphobic behavior: as a disguise for something else. Perhaps unconsciously the woman wants to leave her husband. This thought produces tremendous guilt that arises out of her moral code. She suppresses the urge to leave. The urge is then replaced by a conscious phobia that involves leaving the house. Venturing outside, in the woman's mind, is distorted by guilt and repression. The end result is increasing fear and obsession over actually leaving the house.

A childhood marked by chronic invasion of personal boundaries limits an adult's freedom of association, movement, and making of outside contacts. Such invasions span a wide range from violation of confidences, suppression of differing views, nonacknowledgment of feelings, and the imposition through coercion of irrational beliefs and threats to physical and sexual abuse. Such a childhood, coupled with an overactive imagination, can be a dangerous time bomb.

Trauma is traditionally thought of as a stimulus that overwhelms the ego and produces various symptoms and incapacities in the affected person. But trauma can also be the absence of stimuli—abandonment and neglect.

There are a number of events during infancy and childhood that affect a child's feelings of safety and fear. The availability or disappearance of caretakers both physically and emotionally is one factor. The pleasure and security of being embraced versus being left alone is another. What children are taught about their bodies, their genitalia, and adult treatment of those bodies is critical. What children are taught through actions and words about the roles of men and women is formative.

If a woman's place is in the home, agoraphobia is a woman's form of sit-in protest. It is retreatist separatism, an unwillingness to participate, a refusal to collaborate in any aspect of life. Here is another crippling disease that affects mostly women. Why?

As a culture we collude in the entrapment of women. Women still are not paid equally when they work outside the home. We blame mothers for the bad behavior of their children as if only they—no one and nothing else—influenced their lives. We conspire with rapists and criminals when judges acquit men for crimes against women because of what women wore, where she was at what time, or how much she had had to drink.

Women are sent a continuous and loud message: "It's not safe, it's not safe, it's not safe." The limits placed on women are extensive, and some women, perhaps with added stress and trauma from their past, incorporate these limits into their perceptions of themselves: "It's not safe, it's not safe." In a way, agoraphobia is a metaphor for the historical intimidation and oppression of women. For centuries women have been trained in self-hatred, self-limitation, and self-punishment. When pushed to the extreme, a woman begins to fear being in control. She loses trust in setting her own direction and moving on her own. A sense of boundary and personal safety is so unavailable to her that she feels she has no choice but to seclude herself behind the barrier of the four walls of her home. This woman stops exploring and gives over responsibility for her life. The submission is truly crippling.

SELF-MUTILATION

Self-mutilation is a shocking reality that many people would rather not discuss. I accept the definition of self-mutilation as any harmful or potentially harmful form of nonsuicidal behavior. I place smoking, substance abuse, overeating, and risk taking in the same category with intentional self-defacement and disfigurement.

Direct self-destructive behavior is defined as deliberately causing immediate and concrete physical harm to the body. Indirect self-destructive behavior refers to repetitive forms of behavior that occur over time and cumulatively result in self-harm. With these indirect forms the individual generally fails to acknowledge his self-destructive elements.

Self-mutilative behavior is difficult to understand because it runs counter to the usual human preference for avoiding pain and seeking pleasure. It challenges our beliefs about what pain and pleasure really are. The intent of self-mutilative behavior is to reduce intense feelings of anger, tension, or depression. The process involves loss or threatened loss. The mutilator feels mounting tension but is incapable of expressing it. As the feelings escalate, the mutilator begins to leave his body, to depersonalize and dissociate. The wounding act serves to alleviate the tension, usually without the mutilator feeling pain, and brings him back into the body. In essence, the person creates physical pain that distracts him from emotional feelings that are too painful to bear.

Behavior that is harmful to oneself can be used as a form of self-stimulation, an escape from frightening feelings of emptiness and loss. An expression of self-harm can serve as a means of reducing intolerable tension or venting inexpressible anger. Self-mutilation can also be a way to feel when someone is numb inside. The incidence of self-mutilative behavior has increased

markedly in the past thirty years. It is suspected that
this behavior is still highly underreported.

In some cases self-mutilative behavior has its origin
in culturally acceptable forms of self-alteration. For instance, the grooming of fingernails or hair can become
exaggerated and extreme. The practices of body adornment can get distorted. Ear piercing that covers the entire rim of the ear and earlobe is, to me, an example of
acceptable body adornment gone berserk.

Self-mutilation is considered unrelated to suicide because the motivations are different. Mutilators attack a
particular part of the body in order to produce psychic
relief. A suicide, however, attacks the entire body but
feels the relief beforehand, when the decision is made.

Self-mutilative behavior usually begins during adolescence. Several types of childhood and/or adolescent
experiences may contribute to the development of this
self-injurious behavior. The childhood conditions include the loss of a parent, injury or surgery, physical
and/or sexual abuse, parental violence, and role modeling of impulsive self-destructive behavior within the
family. Three childhood loss experiences that seem
significant for subsequent self-mutilators are (1) placement in foster care, (2) placement in a group home, and
(3) divorce. In each case a separation takes place without permanent termination of the relationship with the
parents. These lingering forms of loss seem to present
an enormous challenge for children to resolve.[4] Each of
these conditions sets the stage for the establishment of
a vulnerability to loss, the establishment of a distorted
or alienated body image, and the modeling of behavior
experienced in the home. Body image problems can be

associated with childhood illness. Children may come to associate pain, disfigurement, or the scarring of surgery with obtaining care and nurturing. A sense of body alienation is also highly characteristic of children who have been sexually abused. There is a high incidence of self-destructive behavior among incest survivors.

Experiences in adolescence that may contribute to the development of self-mutilative behavior include loss of a loved one, peer isolation and conflict, and alienation from the body—the numbing that is described by people who have little or no contact with the feelings of their physical bodies. Teenagers who practice self-mutilation are more likely to have eating disorders, to be inattentive to their physical appearance, to experience sexual identity distress, and to have chronic or serious illnesses.[5] The correlation between self-mutilators and eating disorders is particularly high. Adolescents who have experienced considerable alienation from their bodies during childhood are likely to experience the changes of puberty as threatening and frightening.

It may be that the self-mutilator chooses a certain behavior—wrist cutting, picking, hair pulling, tattooing, burning, or nail biting—because it metaphorically expresses in a single act his childhood losses and boundary violations. In this respect self-mutilation acts out the family secrets and silenced pain.

As in the case of anorexia nervosa, self-mutilators believe their bodies are disgusting, deserving of punishment, and in need of severe management. The body is used as a means of communicating that which is otherwise unexpressible. There is a belief that some action must be taken to reduce unpleasant feelings. All three of these ideas constitute an intrusion on personal boundaries, and each contributes to self-destructive behaviors.

AUTISM

Bruno Bettelheim's book *The Empty Fortress* deals with the issue of infantile autism. In it he presents the theory that the acute withdrawal and isolation associated with autism are an adaptive response to a cold, rejecting attitude on the part of the mother or primary caretaker. When the mother was unconsciously perceived by the infant as not being interested, the child withdrew.[6] Bettelheim's work is generally not held in high esteem these days. Today there is a consensus that autism is due to inborn factors.

Psychoanalyst Alice Miller argues that as a world we collude to protect and condone the behavior of parents toward children, even when such behavior could easily be called abuse. In her book *Banished Knowledge* she tells the story of a woman who took into her home a nine-year-old autistic boy. By giving him plenty of warmth and physical contact, by being available and reacting to him positively, she was able to help him to confirm his feelings and sense his needs. Eventually they began to communicate through signals. In her arms the boy learned how to show emotions, to experience anger at what had been done to him in the past, and to discover love. Ultimately he developed into a healthy, intelligent, fully functioning boy. Miller confronted experts in the field of autism and asked them to explain this phenomenon. Without exception they all continued to argue that autism is an incurable neurophysiological disease and that this boy must have been misdiagnosed.[7] I don't know the answer, but I find the question fascinating from the standpoint of personal boundaries and personal damage.

The examples given in this section are extreme behavioral adaptations in response to overwhelming feelings. There are people who would argue that neurochemistry plays a greater role in determining behavior than does psychology. While I'm sure brain chemistry is involved in everything we do, I do not subscribe to the inevitability of self-destruction. Remember to keep in mind the notion of a continuum—a continuum of boundary invasion as well as a continuum of self-destructive behavior. It is necessary for our personal inventory to ask ourselves some questions. The following are some examples. You will know your own questions.

Do you hate yourself when you eat dessert?
Do you hate yourself when you don't exercise?
Do you wear your seat belt?
Do you speed?
Do you use dental floss regularly?
Do you smoke?
Do you drink?
Do you drink and drive?
Do you eat too much?
Do you eat too little?
Do you scratch bites until they bleed?
Do you scratch your scalp until it is irritated?
Do you pick at blemishes on your face?
Do you chew your lip?

Do you bite your nails?

Do you skydive?

Do you ever say, "I could just kill myself for
_____?"

Do you sometimes hate yourself?

Do you think you are too fat?

Do you care too much what other people think of
you?

Do you have an imagined audience?

Do you know what is best for you?

CHAPTER 3

"No" Is *a* Complete Sentence

$\mathscr{W}$HILE WE WERE GROWING UP MANY OF US HEARD MESsages such as "You can't tell *me* 'no'!" "Children should be seen and not heard." " 'No' is not a complete sentence." "What do you mean, 'no'? 'No' what?" and "Come back when you've figured out what you really want to say." We may have felt ignored or put down. Certainly we were not heard by those with whom we were trying to communicate. The development of healthy, honest communication skills was stunted. Some of us kept on talking longer and louder, desperate for someone to listen, and some of us built thick walls behind which we could hide alone.

I was a wall builder. Whenever the world felt hostile, I would withdraw and put up an emotional barrier. It felt safer behind the walls of my isolation, but sometimes I felt that I was trapped and couldn't get out. My protective defense mechanisms were rigid and inflexible, but I didn't know any other way to try to maintain a sense of safety. Isolation and emotional withdrawal were my only alternatives. As I've gotten older, it has become important to have more alternatives. The walls of my childhood wouldn't let people come in and go out. Through years of awkward attempts to connect with other people, I have been learning lessons about boundaries, limits, and barriers. Today I know that "No" *is* a complete sentence and I can use it whenever I feel the need. I can say "No" selectively and don't have to block out all of my experience in order to feel safe.

I write about the things I need to learn. I write in order to work through and understand my own self-destructive behaviors and thought patterns. For the past several years I have been on a learning journey, learning how to use communication instead of impermeable walls to ensure a sense of personal boundary and safety. Along this journey I have found many people stumbling around with the same confusion: people stifled by guilt, anger, anxiety, shame, and fear; people unaware of their right to set limits and have them respected; people so plagued by their need to be accepted that they have molded themselves into false images. It is for all of us that I share my learning journey.

EXAMPLES

Gail is waiting in line at a bookstore behind a woman whose purchase has necessitated that the cashier go back into the store to look up a price. Gail is not in a big hurry, so she decides to wait. The woman ahead of her keeps apologizing despite Gail's reassurances that there is no problem. A third woman comes up to the counter and reaches between the two women to examine a book on the rack, turns, and places herself in line between them. Gail registers a vague feeling of intrusion, then immediately begins minimizing the situation to herself. She tells herself the woman has only one book, and what difference does it make, anyway? Farther beneath the surface of her mind a voice is screaming for her to stand up for herself: "She cut in line; I don't have to stand for that." The self-sacrificer and the healthy self-asserter within Gail bicker back and forth while she stands immobilized. It turns out that the first woman in line steps in to tell the third woman that Gail was next in line. The woman moves on to another line. The situation is resolved.

I am having breakfast in a local restaurant with a friend, and the waiter is pouring coffee into my cup without asking either of us what we would like to drink. I think, "I don't drink coffee," but I let him pour a whole cup because he was there with the pot already pouring. My friend pipes up without difficulty, "I would like decaf, please."

A friend calls me at 10 P.M. I am in bed reading and wish I had not picked up the phone the second my friend starts talking about the fight he had with his girlfriend. I know from countless experiences that this lament could go on for an hour without my ever saying a word.

I am not listening to my friend as anger and resentment begin boiling in my brain. Thoughts shoot up to

me: "Why does he have to call so late? He knows I go
to bed early!" I am consumed by rage and cannot remember one single reason why I was ever friends with
this guy in the first place. At 11 P.M. we say good-bye,
and I hope it's for the last time. I go to sleep angry at
him and, without knowing it, at myself.

These examples are certainly not life-threatening and
may not appear at first glance to be self-destructive. But
they are glaring examples of the unthinking ways we
sacrifice ourselves for the purpose of avoiding conflict.

I have been making the point throughout this book
that people turn to various self-destructive behaviors
and thought patterns as a means for discharging undesirable feelings. This is reactive behavior and is not necessarily made by free choice. Healing takes place when a
person can discover his or her problems and make real
choices, choices that will positively affect the outcome.

Self-destructiveness can be defined as creating, tolerating, defending, and continuing actions that our conscious mind tells us we do not want to do. Acts of
self-destruction violate what our common sense would
hold is in our best interest. Self-destructive habits and
behaviors are things that cause us shame. We hide our
habits and hide behind them. Where are these attitudes
and beliefs born?

As children, we grow up experiencing people putting
labels on us. We are "Mommy's little helper," "a little
rascal," "just the cutest little thing," or "a good-for-
nothing, stupid little brat." These labels contribute to
the development of our self-images and become part of
how we see ourselves. These labels become etched into

our personalities. How we come to view ourselves through the labels *cute*, *messy*, *precious*, *rotten*, or *selfish* plays a part in our subsequent achievement or failure, happiness or unhappiness. Self-image further affects whether we become assertive or submissive, self-directed or chaotic. In short, the development of self-image during childhood is a critical determinant of our future lives and ability to connect with other people.

Ideally, as we grow and mature, we shed the labels we have carried from childhood and begin to see ourselves through our own eyes and experiences. This is a crucial step in the development of a true identity. Unfortunately, for many of us the early labels remain indelibly etched components of our personality. We remain trapped by images that tell us we are unlovable, unworthy, evil, disliked, and sorry. The labels maintain a self-image that is degrading and relentlessly critical, leaving us vulnerable to the abuse of others and of ourselves. Old messages and descriptions leave us with contaminated self-images with which we struggle, hide ourselves, hate ourselves, and medicate. Unexamined, these labels are the seeds of our self-hatred and self-destruction.

People repeat acts begun in childhood that do not give them pleasure. Repetition of an act tends to perpetuate it, even if the act is harmful or criminal. After a short while, the person becomes indifferent and the act stops feeling wrong. It may even start feeling good. Such acting out may include fighting, promiscuous sexual activity, drug use, nail biting, overeating, hair pulling, smoking, negativism, and constant oppositional behavior. In and of themselves these behaviors do not bring satisfaction, but to children they are a way to express a bottled-up emotion. For adults they are self-destructive habits.

When a person engages in self-damaging behavior, he is violating a standard for his well-being. As the behavior begins, there may be some pain and remorse, but eventually the standard becomes diminished and the feelings subside. With each act the person is rearranging his or her mental state slightly so that subsequent acts seem almost routine. The emotions that originally attended the behavior diminish as the act becomes automatic. Some examples of self-destructive behavior include the following:

Feeling obligated to everyone
Doing more than you want to for other people
Letting other people influence what you do or say
Letting other people influence how you feel about
     yourself
Not accepting or respecting yourself
Being so dependent on the acceptance of others that
     you can't stand up for yourself
Not building significant relationships with other
     people
Imagining a constantly hostile "out there" environ-
     ment
Dwelling on disaster
Hiding
Harboring loads of guilt
Not expressing anger
Unhealthy behaviors: smoking, drinking, using drugs,
     compulsive sexual relationships

Not expecting love and support
Holding excessively critical feelings toward oneself
   and others
Putting oneself at unnecessary risk
Tolerating unnecessary emotional pain
Intentionally antagonizing authority figures

As long as a person's beliefs keep him trapped into thinking that a particular way of being is the only way, that person cannot change. Each day brings the same frame of mind. This set frame of mind does not allow for a change in perspective. For this individual there are no alternatives, no choices. But for those who want to make changes in their thoughts and behavior, reflection and honesty can lead to a new awareness of where changes can be made. The first step in overcoming self-destructiveness is to acknowledge that our thoughts and behavior are not alien. Rather, they are part of our personalities and as such need to be integrated into the whole of our being. It is through acceptance and integration that we facilitate transformation.

Patient observation and mindfulness can create alternative thoughts and beliefs that will increase a person's resources. Later, through an accumulation of experience and right actions, a person can produce a real change in his mental attitude. Finally, a change in attitude affects behavior. The problem lies in believing. Alternative choices need to be seen as feasible before they can be accepted. Unless we believe in the possibility of change, we cannot make it happen.

Consider author Bob Marsenich's outline of the steps of change.

CHANGE

ACCEPTANCE

UNDERSTANDING

AWARENESS

Awareness is the stage where we come to recognize that something is not right or as we might like it to be. This is where we break through the veil of denial that may have been keeping our awareness skewed. Or this may be the point where we finally get all the pieces of information we need to actually know and begin to understand something.

Understanding is the next step in our movement toward change. This is the stage where we investigate our thought, beliefs, and behaviors in order to trace their origins or original purposes. This is where we gather the facts in order to establish an intellectual underpinning for ourselves so that the frightening aspects of change will not overwhelm us. We may need to learn about our upbringing in order to understand why we have the behaviors and attitudes we do. We may need to acknowledge the many subtle ways in which our lives are affected by images in the media. Or we may need to re-examine our responses to and interpretations of our past or present lives. Understanding adds perspective to our experiences and makes it possible to accept ourselves just the way we are.

Acceptance of things as they are at present doesn't mean that you won't try to change them at some point in the future. Acceptance means that you are allowing things to exist right now, just as they are, without the added burden of self-hatred or judgment. Since we all have areas that need attention and improvement, you are better off recognizing and accepting that fact right now.

Change is possible when we have moved through all the previous steps and can begin to imagine alternatives and make new choices for ourselves. Without the first three steps we might try to force ourselves to change something about ourselves, but the change would be coming out of guilt and self-hatred. Therefore, the possibility of the change being in our best interest or being successful is limited.

As I was growing up, conflict and emotional outbursts were responded to by sending the offender to her room. The instructions about what to do while in that room were vague, but it was clear we were being punished for behavior that could not be tolerated in public. The take-home message was to isolate, to go away rather than deal with feelings and/or pursue conflict resolution. While I didn't always like being silenced in this manner, I liked being in my room. It always felt safe behind the closed door. This sort of retreat became my style of coping with confusing emotions and the upsurge of conflict that naturally occurs between people.

I remember feeling angry and frustrated the moment my banishment was pronounced. The entry to my room was usually punctuated with a resounding door slam: my last word. To this day I still have a fantasy of slamming doors with great force and satisfying bangs whenever I feel angry. The behavior is designed to literally shut out whatever is making me mad so that I can avoid experiencing and working through my feelings. I am afraid of anger in myself and in other people, and I want to run away from it. I would rather isolate myself behind the safety of a closed door than confront an angry person. I try to avoid the need to confront conflict and work toward resolution because I don't know how to control that.

Control is a critical issue here. People who do not have a clear sense of personal boundaries and little notion of how to maintain and protect them have a tremendous and almost global need to control the circumstances in their lives. The idea is that if you cannot protect and defend yourself, then you'd better try to control what happens around you. This drive to control the external environment and the ensuing frustration and disappointment we inevitably feel are what lead us to build walls, isolate ourselves, use drugs, become addicted to television, compulsively seek sexual partners, stop eating, and all the other forms of self-destruction people turn to.

A few years ago I identified control as being a major contributor to my isolation and conflict avoidance behaviors. It became clear that I needed to look into establishing some other kinds of boundaries, something a bit more flexible and less self-destructive. My tendency to want to control people, events, and things was making me miserable and destroying my friendships. In the guise of "helping other people," I was wearing myself out and feeling unconnected to anyone. It was time to search out and create new alternatives.

As I have been investigating and researching the issue of boundaries, I have discovered that there are quite a few of us who don't know much about how to set lim-its, say "No," and feel safe. This learning journey is about opening doors and creating a personal boundary that will allow for connection with other people and ul-timately with the community. It is about breaking down walls, ending isolation, breaking destructive or addic-tive patterns, and learning true compassion for oneself and others.

For many years of my life I confused compassionate support with taking care of other people. I had plenty of responsibility, so I extended it outside myself and was overly responsible for others. I had no sense of bound-ary when it came to doing things for other people. I didn't respect my own limits, and I couldn't recognize anyone else's. I created a false sense of connection with others in this caretaking role, while deep below the sur-face of my awareness I secretly felt resentful, used, and very, very tired.

Once I recognized and accepted my mistaken judg-ment, I set about designing a two-part program for self-regulation. I wanted to stop being so automatic in my response to other people's real or perceived needs. To do so I needed to create an alternative response. My first step involved making a pact with myself that I would not even consider doing things for people that they had not specifically asked me to do. This may sound ridiculous, but if you talk to any overachieving caretaker or if you are one yourself, you will know that we are almost physically linked to the wants and desires of other people, even strangers. Those of us who are es-pecially practiced can sense what another person wants or needs before that person even has had a chance to register it. This is the curse of the caretaker.

So I made myself withstand the urge to swoop in and make things better, easier, faster, whatever, until I actually heard a request come out of someone's mouth in a direct manner. I had to stop myself a few times in the beginning from jumping in to fulfill vague requests like "Gee, I would really like to take a vacation sometime this year, but there isn't anyone to work in the store for me" and "I could really use a new typewriter." After a while, and certainly not without some effort, I got the hang of my new program. Then I would consider only a clear, direct request presented specifically to me: "Could you take me to the airport tomorrow?" "Would you take care of my cat while I am out of town?" "May I use your luggage to go to Africa this summer?" That's when I launched into the second step of my program.

In this second and most vital stage I would take a deep breath, let the air out slowly, and reply, "I need a little time to think about that. I'll let you know as soon as I can." It was a bold and daring move for someone used to saying "Yes," "Sure," or "Whatever you want" before a request was ever made. A few of my friends were surprised, but most didn't seem to notice at all. I was terrified the first few times I tried it. I don't know quite what I thought would happen, but the change was unnerving. These were my first deliberate and conscious steps toward setting some limits on my behavior in relation to the real or imagined needs and desires of other people.

Several things happened as a result of this change in my automatic behavior. The first thing was that I lost some friends. Some people found it intolerable when I surprisingly said "No" to something they expected from me. I heard the dreaded label from childhood again—"You are so selfish"—and I cringed. Some people were relieved and told me that they used to feel smothered by me, that I was always taking things out of their hands and "helping" in ways that left them feeling inadequate. For myself, I noticed a huge increase in personal energy. I had more time, attention, and energy to focus on myself and my own wishes and dreams. I no longer felt tired all the time, and resentment disappeared almost completely. I never felt like taking the telephone off the hook because I was so overwhelmed by what everyone needed from me. The phone was no longer the bearer of tasks. Now I could say "No." Another outcome of the change was that I started having more awareness of my feelings. I was suddenly "in touch" with myself. It was scary at first. My self-destructive caretaking behavior had been a convenient way to not have time for myself.

There are other ways, if you do not happen to be a caretaker/controller, in which you may be participating in hiding your feelings from yourself. Believe me, it is a shock when we sneak up behind ourselves and notice the ways in which we are all capable of self-deception. We create delusions for ourselves in order to stay unconnected to our feelings. We may displace them. By this I mean we look outside ourselves for our feelings. This may take the form of constantly seeking approval and affirmation from the outside world. We may strive for perfection and run ourselves into the ground trying to get attention. We may compulsively look for new and exciting sexual partners to boost our egos and give our self-esteem a quick shot in the arm. We may have love affairs with alcohol and drugs, shopping malls and credit cards, racetracks and blackjack tables, ice cream, Brie cheese, and French bread. In short, whenever we look outside ourselves for feelings of gratification or satisfaction, we are looking in the wrong place. It is self-destructive to believe more in what other people tell you about yourself than in what you know already. It is not self-loving to look to others for the proof of your goodness. Furthermore, it is a boundary violation to expect that someone or something else will provide your good feelings.

We may project our feelings onto other people. Usually we do this with the people we are closest to. Perhaps we imagine that our partner is angry. We may prod and poke and stir up a fight just to get our partner to let out the anger when all along the anger is in us. We do not own our feelings when we project them onto others. The act itself represents an attempt to make the other person own what belongs to us. By projecting our feelings onto others we are violating an emotional boundary.

Another way to avoid having any contact with the feelings we have locked away inside is to become so involved in some repetitive behavior that little time and no attention are left over. Maybe we keep the house meticulously neat, keep excellent records neatly filed and cross-referenced, or endlessly train for marathons. Maybe we spend countless hours in front of a video screen playing games or crawl into our computer programs and get lost. Some peole have such a relentless to-do list that they never have a moment for quiet reflection. I have heard these people referred to as "human-doings" as opposed to human beings.

Compulsive thinking is a major co-conspirator in the race to stay ahead of our feelings. If we can pick something—an idea, event, person, anything—and spend all our time thinking about it, we've created the perfect escape. Some people spend all their time worrying; their minds create constant disasters for which they are always preparing. Some people get riveted onto another person to the exclusion of attending to themselves. The anorexic women described in the last chapter spend inordinate amounts of time obsessing about thinness, their bodies, and food. Women with agoraphobia must have internal worlds that produce enough fear to keep them paralyzed within their homes.

In extreme cases, when the need to avoid feelings is perceived as being crucial for survival, a person may produce somatic symptoms that limit his perception of the world. Examples include hysterical blindness, deafness, and paralysis. It is thought that multiple personalities come forth when the ego is presented with more than it can cope with. Multiple personalities, rather than limiting the person's ability to act, actually make it possible for that individual to survive. But certainly the splitting of the personality can be considered a way to keep unbearable feelings hidden.

Repressing, hiding, swallowing, or stuffing our feelings causes us physical and emotional damage and is therefore another form of self-destructiveness. Marilyn described herself to me:

I used to throw up a lot. I thought it was because I was so high-strung. I would just get anxious, and then I'd be sick. But since I have been getting in touch with my anger and my fear and have been able to talk about them instead of swallowing them all the time, I never throw up anymore.

The results of staying out of touch with our feelings can be seen in low self-respect, feelings of shame, social anxiety and unease, the inability to assert oneself, the inability to ask for or receive emotional support, the inability to express love, the inability to express anger until it has become full-blown rage, and the likelihood of feeling exploited by other people. Each of these symptoms is an example of boundary damage and the subsequent limited ability to protect oneself.

Families teach their members about feelings and their expression or repression. Some families encourage the expression of emotion, and do not censor certain ones in favor of others. The language of emotions is used in these families and is taught to the children. Children and their experiences are treated as valuable. Parents support their children's understanding of and reactions to the world. Emotional, physical, and spiritual boundaries are respected and nurtured in these families.

Then there is the looking-good family that has already been described. In this family, certain emotions are discouraged and the children are trained in the value of propriety at all costs. Reality becomes twisted and distorted in order to preserve the projected image of this perfect family. Emotions that ruffle the calm waters of the family are squelched. Emotional and intellectual boundaries are not respected in these families.

There are abusive families who use degrading words or a slap in the face to express feelings and resolve conflicts. Rather than being repressed, anger and pain are amplified in these families. Children cannot learn to defend themselves adequately. They often grow into adults who feel like helpless victims. But they also grow into adults who have been trained to use brutality and violence to solve their problems. Physical, emotional, and spiritual boundaries are routinely violated in these families.

In contrast to the abusive family, there is the family that seems to have shut off emotions completely. Family members are cool and unresponsive to one another. Conflict cannot emerge in this environment. Actually this family is equally abusive; it is just harder to see it. In this family the child is virtually ignored by parents who are unable or unwilling to be emotionally available. The child learns that he has no influence, no power, can make nothing happen. The child feels rejected and grows into an adult who is virtually unable to evaluate the feelings of other people. This is a terrifying and defenseless way to feel.

Next there is the family whose rules are laid down and enforced by the iron fist of guilt. Compliance among family members is attained through threat, criticism, comparison, and the relentless prediction of disastrous outcomes: "You'll never be any good," "Why can't you be more like John?" "Your father will have something to say about this when he gets home." The taunts go on and on. Akin to this is the family that uses the wrath of God like a rigid whip to keep members in line. When religion is used in this punitive manner, spirituality is lost. When beliefs become punitive, rigid, and exclusive, true spirituality has been violated.

Feelings and conflict are normal and inevitable outcomes of human interaction. Rather than accepting this fact, people label them "good" or "bad" and accept or reject them accordingly. A human price is paid whenever certain feelings or conflicts are denied and repressed. A complete absence of conflict can be found only in people who have been frightened or threatened to the point of docility or whose minds have been deadened by some sort of brainwashing.

It is within these various types of family, or a blending of any of them, that each of us has learned lessons about how, when, where, which, and to whom we can express our feelings. Let's take a look some of the feelings that often get distorted.

ANGER AND PAIN

Anger is probably the most universally suppressed emotion in our culture. No one gets much permission to express this emotion, least of all women. If this emotion has not been repressed completely in you, chances are that it has been twisted somehow. Lee told me:

I used to have this image of my mom, and it still hasn't gone away completely. She'd be standing in front of me, and I'd know she was angry. Then she'd open her mouth like the door to a furnace, and flames would shoot out and I would be roasted on the spot before her. I get this image whenever I think about anger. It scares me.

Anger is part of human nature. Quite possibly anger is the earliest emotion we experience. Anger is not something we learn or something that we choose to participate in just to get attention. Anger is a response to pain. Anger is life-affirming; it calls for change. We are taught to suppress both pain and anger, and the result is the epitome of self-destruction. Without awareness of pain and anger, how can we possibly protect ourselves?

Depending on how we saw anger handled in our families, we may have learned that it is appropriate to lash out, to humiliate, to punish or destroy others with our anger. Or we may have learned that no matter how others treat us, even if they abuse us, we have no right to defend ourselves with anger. Our past experiences with anger have distorted a healthy sense of personal boundary.

Thus, it is our early experiences with anger—how others respond to our anger, what we are told about it, how we see others handle the emotion—that shape our ability to defend and protect ourselves.

Anger is a signal that something is wrong, that a boundary has been violated, that safety and well-being are being compromised. Some common experiences that can trigger anger include the following:

Humiliation
Not being respected
Not being listened to

Having one's motives incorrectly assigned by some-
   one else
Being told what you "should" do
Being insulted
Being belittled
Being ignored
Being deceived
Being rejected
Being crowded
Having one's mind read
Having assumptions made about oneself
Feeling controlled by someone else

Holding back anger prevents us from dealing with the
real issues within ourselves and with other people.
Holding back anger does not, as many would like to believe, eliminate it. On the contrary, holding back anger
only makes it grow and become unpredictable. Held
too long, anger can explode as rage and abuse. Held too
long, it can turn back onto itself as depression. Sarcasm
and cynicism are often used to disguise anger, but they
are anger just the same.

People without "No" feel helpless and powerless.
They are trapped and angry, whether they recognize it
or not. Learning how to express and use anger as a
method for setting boundaries is a way to become honest with ourselves and with those around us. Identifying
your style is a discovery. You will need to do so to
break free. Do you recognize yourself as one of the following types?

The Rock

You keep quiet when something bothers you. You are strong. You don't want to make trouble: "Don't rock the boat." "Be a grown-up about this." You deny any so-called negative feelings such as anger. You let other people take advantage of you, even mistreat you at times. On the outside you look relaxed. Inside, you suffer.

The Time Bomb

You hold on to your anger until you explode. You store things up so that by the time you can react, you are at the ends of your rope. You procrastinate in taking care of yourself. People with this style often have physical illnesses, headaches, ulcers, and insomnia as a result of holding everything inside. Frequently, people with this style are also verbally if not physically abusive.

The Martyr

You are afraid of making other people mad. You want everything to be in harmony at any cost. You hold on to your anger in order to avoid conflict. You constantly apologize and use vague language to disguise the situation and your feelings. Your communication is indirect, using tone of voice, a look, hints, and sighs to get your needs met. You wish others were as sensitive to you as you are to them.

The Whiner

You are easily annoyed. You anticipate problems—the job done wrong, the price too high, the inevitable disappointment. You are impatient. Lots of things bother you. You complain, confront, and nag. You make a fuss over things that others can ignore. You are difficult to be around.

The Rigid Scaredy-Cat

You are concerned only with yourself. You draw conclusions before having all the information. You cannot believe that anyone else has your interests at heart. You do not take the time to consider options or the opinions of others. You speak and act without thinking. You are scared to get close to other people. You use anger and abrasiveness to harshly exclude others from your life in an attempt to feel safe.

The Judge

You are aggressive, stubborn, abrasive, and downright rude in your pursuit of what you want. You are demanding in what you say and how you say it. You are condemning of other people. You think in absolutes: "She will never . . ." "He always . . ." Your mind works overtime creating private catastrophes. You are sometimes accused of being a borderline personality.

Any of these styles appears undesirable when examined by itself. They are the extremes, the strategies taken too far. Establishing healthy boundaries involves being able to find the flexible balance between "Yes" and "No." Remember, anger is not the only emotion that can be used in the process of establishing boundaries, it just may be the emotion that first signals that you need to.

ANXIETY

Anxiety is another emotion whose primary experience occurs in early childhood, usually as a result of separation from a primary caretaker. The experience is intense for an infant whose survival depends entirely on the caretaker's presence. Subsequently, situations that re-create feelings of separation anxiety are experienced as so threatening that they can overwhelm the individual. The experience feels like a threat to survival even if in actuality survival is not threatened.

Threats to self-esteem are also a major source of anxiety. The essence of anxiety is the intrusion of distress into one's physical or mental well-being. This intrusion can be real or imagined, but the effect is the same. Anxiety is the result of boundary violation, and it can lead us to all sorts of unhealthy behaviors in order to avoid feeling it.

Anxiety can be disguised as insomnia, bad dreams, excessive alertness, preoccupation, sudden intrusive ideas and fears, physical sensations, waves of emotion that well up and subside, and persistent thoughts we cannot control or stop. The thoughts and feelings associated with anxiety are unpleasant, and most of us try to avoid them. To lessen anxiety we distract our attention. We protect ourselves from anxiety by creating a blind spot in our awareness. This blind spot is the seat of our self-deception, the soothing inattention of denial. It is where we hide our self-hatred, and it is how we feed our self-destructiveness.

The symptoms of denial include the inability to make associations between cause and effect. Denial convinces us that our patterns of behavior are different, healthier, better than they used to be, when in fact they are just the same. "Yes ... but" is frequently heard when our perception is skewed by denial. In denial our emotions are numbed, our responses flattened, and our thoughts constricted. Alternatives are not available when we have limited our scope with denial. We lose the ability to be flexible. Our memories fail us, and we avoid reality by escaping into fantasy. In denial we violate our own boundaries by not staying and confronting the feelings and situations surrounding anxiety.

SHAME

Shame is a feeling we have when we feel that people are aware that we have not lived up to their expectations. Here we are again displacing our sense of self-worth onto the expectations, real or imagined, of other people. We put the love of others above the love of ourselves, then hold ourselves responsible for not attaining it. Any time we step out of the self like that, we are violating a personal boundary. Then, as if that weren't enough, when we fail to get the affirmation we seek from outside, we turn anger and frustration back on ourselves and get depressed.

Many professionals in the mental health field currently believe that issues of unresolved shame are a primary catalyst for self-destructiveness. People striving to avoid the anxiety of separation, the pain of abandonment, loss, and rejection, turn to self-punishment as a way to feel connected. Addictive behaviors gratify and punish at the same time. Carla Wills-Brandon has suggested that addictions serve as parent substitutes. Shame can be an addiction and can sustain other addictive behaviors.

Feeling that we are "no good," that something is basically wrong with us, is shame. This pervasive cloud causes us to doubt ourselves, compulsively seek approval, fear offending others and being abandoned by them, and punish ourselves before a harshly critical internal audience. It is only when we can begin to interrupt this self-hating rebuke that we can start to get out from under the cloud of shame.

GUILT

Guilt is a sense that we are less than what we are supposed to be. It is a relentless prod that urges us to do more and do better. Guilt is a spiritual boundary violation that obscures and destroys our own uniqueness. Guilt leaves us vulnerable to abuse, prevents us from establishing healthy boundaries, and contributes to destructive relationships. It drives us to constantly look outside ourselves for affirmation.

Guilt also works to distract us from other, truer feelings. For instance, we are feeling angry at someone but know that we are not supposed to feel anger, so we feel guilty. Or we are attracted to a particular person, but our religious training has taught us that to lust is a sin, so we feel guilty. Maybe we are afraid to participate in a particular activity, but because other people don't seem to be scared, we push ourselves to do things we don't want to do. On the other hand, if we respect our fear and refuse to participate, we feel guilty. Guilt is defi-

nitely one of the ways we disrespect ourselves and violate our boundaries.

Some self-destructive behaviors that are sponsored by
guilt include the following:

Overcommitment and the compulsive need to help
     others
Always wondering how others perceive us
Constantly apologizing for ourselves
Comparing ourselves with others
Worrying about being selfish
Not asking for help
Pushing ourselves with "must" and "should"
Being unable to say "No"

Guilt was the way you were manipulated into compliance as a child. You were parented with guilt. As a result of this sort of upbringing, guilt became a
mechanism incorporated in your brain, automatic and
constant. Guilt was fostered with childhood put-downs
like "You are selfish," "You think you are so smart,"
and "You're such a bad kid." These messages are taken
in so thoroughly during childhood that they are difficult
to search out and exorcise when we are adults. Guilt
prevents self-love and is therefore destructive.

As we grow up, we learn from our families and from
the culture that certain aspects of who we are and how
we feel are intolerable. So whenever any of those aspects surface, we have to keep them hidden. Just as society punishes the thing it cannot tolerate, we learn to
punish ourselves as well. Guilt is part of this punishment.

Living with and nourishing an invisible but ever-present enemy is a drain on our energy. It saps our resources and obscures the possibilities for change.

On the more positive side, guilt, like anger, can direct our attention to areas in ourselves where problems exist. In this case guilt is not irrational and obliterating; it is illuminating. Rather than trapping us into a relentless cycle of self-punishment, guilt can point to where changes need to be made.

FEAR

Fear is a signal that something is wrong, that there is danger present, and that something needs to be done to protect oneself. Fear is a natural and self-protecting emotion. But as with anger, we are taught not to acknowledge fear. Men are particularly targeted as children: "Don't be a baby," "Fraidy cat, fraidy cat!" and "Big boys aren't afraid of the dark." We learn to disguise fear as other emotions or act it out through various behaviors.

For many years I was completely separated from the emotion of fear. I literally did not have a word for it. I disguised the emotion as anger. Whenever my sense of well-being was threatened, I would fly into a rage. I would condemn and criticize and spew venom far and wide. It was through the process of reconnecting with the frightened child inside myself and learning how to reassure and protect her that I was able to accept and honor my fears while continuing to attempt to create safety.

Anxiety is an example of vague fear, while phobias

are strong fears of specific objects or situations. Phobias are excessive and seemingly out of proportion to their circumstances. Excessive fears can totally disrupt a life and disable a person. Agoraphobia is one example of the limiting effects of excessive fear. Racism and homophobia are larger manifestations of the destructiveness that can come from fear.

Anger, anxiety, shame, guilt, and fear are the notorious "negative" emotions that people are told are "bad" and "shouldn't be expressed." Therein lies another seed of our self-destructiveness. Feelings are feelings, just that. While some may feel better than others, none ought to be eliminated. Trying to do so is a boundary violation and an intrusion on our selves. Feelings are like moods. They are brought about in various ways, they remain present for a while, and they pass. It is when we begin interfering with this normal ebb and flow that we start doing damage to ourselves and others. We can make changes in our reactions to events and can change our behaviors, but we must stop trying to squash down and eliminate our feelings. Feelings bring us information just as the senses of smell, sight, taste, touch, and hearing do. If you smelled something bad, you wouldn't cut off your nose or stop breathing. If you tasted something you didn't like, you would know not to try it again. Try establishing a relationship with your feelings like the one you have with your senses. Feelings are our allies, not our enemies.

I had an opportunity recently to generate and utilize an alternative behavior. I was writing at my desk one morning, undisturbed and concentrating, when the dogs started barking. I ignored them for a while. When it didn't stop, I left my desk to see who was in the yard. A man in a shirt and tie, carrying a clipboard, was hovering at the bottom of the stairs. He introduced himself as the insurance agent, there to inspect the house ... and could he please come inside to have a look at the woodstove as well.

I felt my throat tighten, which I have learned to recognize as a sign of irritation. I do not like being intruded on without warning, especially when I am writing. My first impulse was to show anger and tell him to leave. Then I recognized this as an opportunity to try another approach. I decided to try honesty and limit setting instead of slamming the door in his face. I told him that it would be fine if he did the inspection but that he was interrupting me at work. He would have to come in to check the stove first so that I could get back to my writing. I acknowledged the irritation to myself and did not have to take it out on him. Instead, I stated a clear limit within which I could be comfortable. He was perfectly agreeable, I did not have to act like a shrew, and both of our needs were met.

As he came up the stairs I was hit by the strong smell of men's cologne. I have a very acute sense of smell and find most manufactured scents to be offensive. He reached his hand out to shake mine, and I knew as soon as we touched that I would have that smell on me. It flashed like a meteor through my mind that it would be rude to refuse his handshake; what would he think? Then, just as quickly, I decided I didn't care. I looked him straight in the eye, smiled, and said, "Come on in," completely avoiding looking down at his outstretched hand.

The experience took only a few moments, but I learned several new skills, and when he was gone, he was really gone. I was not left harboring fuming resentment and anger. My ability to feel my feelings and at the same time take care of myself instead of someone else was increased by that experience. I stayed within my own boundary and took care of myself instead of lashing out and invading his boundary.

People need to know what constitutes a boundary violation for them. Not everyone is equally bothered by smell or noise or interruption. Some people find a certain level of stimulation desirable, while others find it unbearable. Boundaries can be compromised by either intrusion or abuse, and it is important to know the difference. The following are some examples of generally accepted invasive behavior that may be, but need not be, tolerated without question.

INTRUSION

Smells

Noise

Interrupting

Violating privacy: reading a journal or letter or going through private spaces (e.g., purse, desk, medicine cabinet)

Lecturing people on things that are important to you but about which they have not asked

Not asking if someone has the time to listen

Finishing someone's thoughts or sentences

Borrowing without permission
Neglect
Urging

INTRUSION ↔ ABUSE

Comparison
Smoking around people who do not smoke
Having high expectations for other people
Violating confidences
Lying
Gossiping
Being told how to dress and wear your hair by a person you have not asked for advice.
Merging personal and professional and public life when doing so is not comfortable
Speculating about someone else's lifestyle
Borrowing without permission and not returning the borrowed item
Not honoring someone's request for personal space
Finishing someone else's thoughts and sentences
Neglect
Urging
Inducing guilt
Criticizing

ABUSE

Comparison
Name-calling
Ignoring or suppressing children's feelings
Physical violence

Emotional violence
Sexual abuse
Sexual harassment—innuendo
Violating privacy—voyeurism
Pollution
Shaming
Destroying others' property
Lying
Neglecting
Inducing guilt
Criticizing

Long before I knew I needed to learn about personal boundaries, I had a friend named Diane who had the most magical phrase that she could make work for her. I will never forget it. She would calmly state, "This is unacceptable." She could look anyone straight in the eye and state her unwillingness to accept less than what she wanted, asked for, or anticipated. There was nothing else to be said in those moments, no possible retort from the recipient, and no groveling from my friend. She was not shaming or verbally accosting the person with whom she spoke. She was just delivering a clear message that something would have to change.

I marveled at this phrase, as I did with the "I don't want to talk about that right now" phrase. Over the years I have collected others. It's sort of like a phrase book for a foreign country; you need to know how to say certain essential things without too much embellishment. Here is a sampling of some of the phrases I have come up with over the years.

"This isn't a very good time for me."

"I really don't want to talk about this right now."

"I want to spend time with you, but I don't want to go to _____."

"The quote you gave me is unacceptable; is that the bottom line?"

"This workmanship is not up to my standard; please redo it."

"No, I don't drink coffee. Do you have any tea?"

"No, I don't want to have sex with you."

"I have only ten minutes for this conversation, and then I will have to hang up."

"I think we have exhausted this subject. I have nothing more to say."

"I've enjoyed our visit, but it is time for you to go now."

"This isn't a good time to get together, but let's make a plan for the future."

"I'm glad you're coming for a visit, and I'll make a hotel reservation for you."

"No, I can't do that for you."

"I need to take care of myself."

"No, smoking is not permitted in my house."

"I'm angry with your behavior."

"I find that remark offensive."

Please feel free to add your own. Take what you need and leave the rest. Remember, you are entitled to the following rights and considerations without any explanation or justification. If you aren't experiencing the total bill of rights, you may be suffering abuse.

BILL OF RIGHTS

I have the right to say "No."

I have the right to determine how and when people enter my space.

I have the right to my feelings.

I have the right to change my feelings without explanation.

I have the right to make choices in my life.

I have the right to follow my own values and standards of behavior.

I have the right to make my own decisions.

I have the right to determine and prioritize my needs and desires.

I have the right to have my needs and wants respected by others.

I have the right to terminate a conversation with anyone who puts me down or is not listening to me.

I have the right to make mistakes and not be perfect.

I have the right to be honest even if it isn't what the other person wants to hear.

I have the right to be angry even at someone I love.

I have the right to feel scared and to say, "I'm afraid."

I have the right to my own personal space and time.

I have the right to be flexible.

I have the right to be in a nonabusive environment.

LAURIE

In his controversial book on infantile autism, *The Empty Fortress*, Bruno Bettelheim tells the story of a young girl named Laurie that clearly illustrated for me the importance and sacredness of personal boundaries.

He describes the girl as a seven-year-old mute autistic with severe anorexia who had not spoken in more than four years. She was locked within herself in a world where no one could go, and into which she would put nothing. She was completely shut down. Before she decompensated into the inertia that brought her to the hospital for treatment, the only spontaneous activities she engaged in were destructive. She liked to tear things up.

With constant attention and intense work on the part of the hospital staff, Laurie slowly began exploring her world again. She started to eat and to make sounds. After many months she slowly and cautiously began taking tiny steps back into the world. In a sense she began to thaw from a deep emotional and physical freeze, but she still did not acknowledge the presence of other people. She was frightened and deeply distrustful of anything she perceived as an intrusion.

Laurie's first purposeful activities (which Bettelheim described as self-assertion) involved ritualistically coloring and tearing paper into long strips, with which she then created a personal boundary wherever she was. Her possession of a world of her own and her existence within it were so precarious for her that any intrusion destroyed them. She set about creating a boundary within which she could exist in safety.

From then on daily, and for hours, she worked with utter abandon and intensity, tearing paper sheets into single continuous strips. These she used for laying new boundaries, but always in such a way that she remained inside the area marked off by these self-created boundaries.[2]

As her ego began to develop, she engaged in the struggle between mastering internal pressures and external reality. The creation of boundaries was her first spontaneous, deliberate activity and a symbolic statement of her concerns.

Creating boundaries within which to feel safe became an elaborate ritual with rigid specifications. She would color the paper for hours before tearing it methodically into strips. Starting at the outside edge, and without even looking at the paper, she would carefully and meticulously tear the paper in descending squares until she reached the center. Stretched out, the paper measured as much as twenty feet. As Laurie's world expanded, so did her territory, and her boundaries reflected this. When she moved to the play yard outside of the hospital she used sand or bark to mark elaborate sine curve boundaries along a seventy-foot ledge at the hospital. Such marking was her nonverbal way of demarcating a boundary and attempting to create an area of safety for herself.

Laurie's story was a concrete example of the process that everyone goes through to create a place of personal safety within the world. Here was a small child, so damaged and ill as to have retreated from the world almost entirely, making a courageous and highly creative attempt to make the world seem safe enough for her to live in. Her way was to create a personal boundary. I loved her story.

CHAPTER 4

The Sharing-Impaired

*H*AVE YOU EVER MET SOMEONE WHO WITHIN THE FIRST few minutes of conversation tells you more about himself than you think you ought to know? Perhaps he has shared intimate details regarding his health, relationships, or finances. Maybe he has asked you personal questions that make you feel uneasy. This person seems to have a high need for closeness and wants to get to know you right away. Have you ever walked away from a first meeting feeling overwhelmed, maybe even a little smothered?

Then there is another kind of person whom you may have known for months and still don't know much about. This person has the need for a lot of space and is reluctant to make plans in advance. He doesn't like to be pinned down and questioned. You have to pull information out if you want to know anything. This person never calls to initiate getting together and usually says "I don't care" to queries about what he wants to do. Getting to know this person is hard work.

These are two extremes of how many people communicate and operate in the world. These extreme styles are what I call the *sharing-impaired*, those who rush into intimacy and share too much too soon and those who are overly cautious, slow, and guarded. Most people fall somewhere between these two extremes but will identify more or less with one or the other style. Whichever style a person has affects the ways in which that person communicates with others.

Communication is perhaps the most important and difficult activity human beings must engage in. It is a delicate membrane through which people can share their thoughts, ideas, feelings, dreams, and sorrows. Communication is a crucial component in human interaction.

Communication is thought to have been successful when it has led to a greater understanding among human beings. When a relationship has improved, communication has worked. If, however, confusion, distortion, misunderstanding, and suspicion have been stirred up, communication has not been successful. While it is possible to use communication to stir up hostility and break down trust, its ideal use is to remove the barriers of misunderstanding that keep people separated. Through honest communication, people can share and learn to honor their differences.

Even though communication is vital, rules for how to do it well are neither taught nor practiced. Is it any wonder that people have trouble understanding one another?

This chapter intends to explore some of the ways in which communication gets distorted and how this distortion can be construed as either intrusion or abandonment. How people receive communication is not always in alignment with the intentions of the sender. We cannot determine how what we say will be heard no matter how carefully we speak. Usually we feel hurt and disappointed when someone misunderstands what we have said, but how they hear us is not within our control. Inside each person's mind lies a vast repository of memories, impressions, labels, and pain left over from childhood. Jamie says to Alan, "Please don't interrupt me when I am on the telephone unless it is an emergency." This seems like a pretty straightforward bit of communication. Well, Alan hears, "Don't ever bother me again, you are a pest, and I am mad at you." He responds defensively to Jamie's request because he is feeling attacked. And considering what he believes he heard, he *has* been attacked. The only problem is that he didn't hear what was communicated; he heard some hyped-up version that passed through his memory. In this way a simple request may turn into a battle.

When people miscommunicate and have their feelings hurt or their expectations disappointed, they tend to respond according to their characteristic style. Some people approach and want more contact, while others withdraw and may build walls. To the one who backs off, someone's approach and need to talk will feel intrusive and clingy, causing him to back off even further. For the one who approaches, withdrawal feels like chilly abandonment and he may feel a sense of panic or acute loss. Both parties feel hurt or disappointed, but they need not continue inflicting pain by misinterpreting each other.

EXAMPLES

I am on an airplane, and the passenger beside me wants to talk. He has asked me what I am reading, what time it is, and where I live. Despite my efforts to ignore him, he is determined to engage me in conversation. He is intruding on my boundaries, and I am feeling annoyed.

I call a friend to ask about her trip to Greece. Forty-five minutes later I have heard the details of the travel agent's ineptitude, the problems with lost baggage at the airport in Athens, and an energetic diatribe on the drivers in Greece, and still I know nothing about the sights, smells, sounds, and tastes that were experienced by my friend. I am exhausted and irritable when we hang up.

My neighbor, who has been planning a long trip for several months, calls me from the airport on her way out of town to ask me to please empty the garbage at her house. It is no big deal to do it for her, but I feel imposed on by the fact that she asked me at the very last minute and I don't feel that "No" was much of an option.

These scenarios are examples of the problems that can come up when people are trying to communicate. The first example illustrates how attempts at conversation can be intrusive when both parties are not equally interested in the pursuit. When both people are willingly engaged, details and questions can be seen as signs of interest and intimacy. When both people are not equally involved, such interest feels invasive and annoying.

The second example is an illustration of how in conversation we sometimes give details that have not been requested. Such unwanted details are received with annoyance because attending to them requires more work than the listener had bargained for or is willing to expend. The second example also illustrates how expectations can sneak in and foul up communication. I had called my friend with the expectation of hearing the positive experiences of her trip. I had not bargained on hearing the annoying and negative aspects. As it turned out, my expectation made it impossible for me to be supportive of and attentive toward whatever my friend chose to share.

The third example is manipulative in its design, but not intentionally so. It would never have occurred to my neighbor that I would say "No" to her request, and in fact the request was minimal. The manipulation comes in because my friend never asked for this favor during the lengthy preparations for her trip. Perhaps she never anticipated this last-minute detail, but the truth of the matter is that she didn't give me much choice because she had chosen to cut the time element so short.

PEER RELATIONS

A peer relationship is one in which both people give and take and both share equal power within the relationship. An unbalanced relationship is one in which one person always takes and the other always gives, one person is constantly needy and the other feels burdened, or one has more power and control.

Sadly, intimate partners are not always peers. When peerness in a relationship has been lost, communication is destined for a rocky ride. One example of how a couple can slip out of peer alignment occurs when one partner asserts himself as the expert, the "I know what's best for you" syndrome that so many with faltering self-esteem may revert to. It's what I talked about in Chapter 2. We put ourselves one up on someone so that we can bolster our sense of self. But in this maneuver we also must leave someone in the position of one down. If we have a partner who doesn't object to this, we are not in a peer relationship. Some other people deliberately put themselves in the one-down position. They may intentionally act dependent because it makes them feel cared for. Or they may believe that it boosts their partner's ego and that it is their job to ego boost. Whatever the motivation, this behavior does not establish a peer relationship. Relationships that are out of peer alignment force feelings to be denied, specifically the feeling of anger.

Peer relationships are difficult for people with damaged boundaries to assess. When we compulsively put other people's needs and feelings ahead of our own, we are not being peers. As we begin to change this pattern, we need role models for healthy peer relationships. Friendship is a good place to begin identifying some of the healthy qualities in a relationship. Usually friendships are not muddied by the same expectations and/or history that are characteristic of a lover or family relationship. When a friendship is not based on true peerness, one participant or both eventually feel let down, drained, deprived, or just plain dissatisfied and will generally back off. But friendships that have been sustained over time and distance are usually healthy relationships that contain many of the desirable elements of peerness.

Giving of yourself to someone who does not give in return is not taking care of yourself. It is not maintaining a reasonable boundary. Such behavior can leave you feeling used, deprived, and even resentful. If you are still operating under the old family label "You are selfish," there is a good chance that you set up just this kind of relationship. It is difficult for people with damaged boundaries to see the differences between what people say to them—"I'm your friend"—and what those same people's actions say—"So I talk about you behind your back."

Being taken care of, pitied, talked down to, and treated like a child or an object on a regular basis is indicative of a nonpeer relationship. When we allow others to objectify us (Daddy's little girl, such a hunk, your show pony), we relinquish our personhood, and we can be easily dismissed when we are not treated as people. When we are overly submissive, we are not protecting the boundary of our individuality. It is crucial that we reclaim our subjectivity, that we remain human beings in the eyes of others.

Domination is the other side of this boundary equation. Taking care of others, pitying, talking down to people, and treating grown-up people like children are disrespectful and unloving. These styles of communicating, putting oneself one up or one down, are asymmetrical styles and will not promote the establishment of a peer relationship. When someone is constantly trying to prove a point instead of sharing with you, there is a good chance that your relationship is not one of peers. Urging, trying to change someone's mind, and lecturing without mutual consent are all forms of boundary violation.

In her book *Intimate Partners* Maggie Scarf addresses the issue of peerness in love relationships this way:

> A very different and much healthier style of loving does not require me to carry one side of my partner's unlovable dilemmas, but to respect his right to handle his dilemmas in his own way, as best he can. I can empathize with him, sympathize with him, support him in his efforts to deal with his problems and difficulties. But loving precludes my trying to take over any part of his inner pain and assuming that he cannot handle it by himself.[1]

This quote is a stunning example of what it takes to keep a balance of peerness in either friendship or love.

A few years ago I was investigating what ingredients go into having a peer relationship with another person. I began examining various important relationships throughout my life to try to understand whether they had been hierarchical or peer. Teachers, parents, and, sadly, most of my romantic relationships fell into the hierarchical category. I began to suspect that the lack of peerness was a root cause for the demise of those intimate relationships and several of my close friendships.

Finally, I discovered a true peer, a friend from high school with whom I am still very close. What has made our friendship different? What are the ingredients that make us peers?

I started my examination with lifestyle. At the time she was married; I was not. She has children; I do not. She lives in a city; I live in the country. She knows all about art; I do not. Obviously we had each chosen different paths, but we dearly love each other despite those differences. What about values? Here I found much more similarity. We hold many of the same values; our lives are guided by many of the same basic beliefs. I also found that even in those areas where we disagree, we respect our differences rather than feel threatened by them. This acceptance and respect allow us to tell each other anything without fearing censure and judgment. We don't give each other advice unless it is asked for, and we don't tell each other how to do things. We trust in each other's competence and take an interest in our individual styles. There is no competition between us and no urge to change one another. Our friendship is surrounded by unconditional acceptance and plenty of love. We can accept each other's differences without having to judge and label them as right and wrong, superior and inferior. They can just be different without causing conflict between us. Differences may look like conflict, but they can be tolerated.

Peerness requires symmetry, balance, and equality. With this in mind, let's look at some other common styles of interaction that are out of balance and most certainly interfere with communication.

CROSS-CULTURAL COMMUNICATION

A couple I know have a regular argument that on the surface looks like it revolves around the issue of details. The woman will ask a simple question to which she wants a short, simple answer. The man will approach the answer from the perspective of history, launching into a discourse that begins somewhere just after the dawn of civilization. Within a very few minutes she interrupts and asks her original question again, explaining that that is all she really wants to know right now. He does not like being interrupted and feels that she isn't interested in all the things he knows and is trying to share with her. He feels rejected and silenced. He acts angry. She feels that he has not listened to her question and is taking the opportunity to give a lecture she doesn't need. She acts angry. The fight is off and running from there.

Deborah Tannen wrote a fascinating book, *You Just Don't Understand*, in which she examines the different styles men and women use to communicate. I have for many years had the suspicion that men and women come from different planets. Even though we use the same words and sentences, we are speaking very different languages. Well, Dr. Tannen has confirmed my suspicion. Her premise is that boys and girls are raised in separate worlds with separate ways of relating and communicating, almost like separate cultures. Then, as men and women, we continue to operate out of those separate worlds and naturally interpret the words and actions of the other gender through the filter of our own training. This filter is one of the ingredients in the vast repository of information scramblers that interfere with communication.

Dr. Tannen argues that we must come to see and accept the different styles in which men and women relate rather than continue to condemn or try to change them. By critically applying the standards of one gender to the interpretation of the behavior of the other gender we are violating boundaries. We are not seeing and embracing the uniqueness of each other.[2]

In the case of the couple who fight when she wants an answer and he wants to share a wealth of information, Dr. Tannen would explain that women are comfortable asking for information and sharing information, while men respond to requests for information with the belief that they must resolve something, offer advice or expertise. Men do not hear a question as a request for information. Men are thrown into the role of protector by a request for information from a woman. Women, on the other hand, when put into the role of protectee, feel they are victims of condescending behavior. This is the moment when peer status has been lost, and here is where the tension lies. If men and women could learn to accept their different styles, it would lessen the struggle and pain associated with feeling we have not been heard. We all want to be heard and understood for what we think we are saying and what we know we mean. In this couple the man is merely trying to be helpful, to give as much information as he can because he believes information is useful. The woman, by contrast, just wants the short question she asked to be answered. Once she has that missing piece of information, perhaps she can listen more generously to all the other things he wants to share. But until she gets what she asked for, she believes she has been ignored.

Dr. Tannen explains how women operate out of a need for peerness and connection with other people, which necessitates cooperation and a minimum of conflict. Little girls play in groups in which everyone appears to have equal status. Adult women in groups seek consensus among the members rather than pick leaders. Men, however, operate from a hierarchical position that requires competition, confrontation, and status. Little boys play in groups that have a leader who tells the others what to do. Adult male functioning in the world looks remarkably similar. For females, talking is the stuff that relationships are made of. For men, doing things is what being with someone else is all about. No wonder communication gets confused between these two cultures.

Men and women hold different values. *Values* are the attitudes toward life that guide our actions in relation to money, sex, religion, politics, safety, status, you name it. Women tend to seek approval and avoid conflict. They are motivated by the need to be liked, and they believe on a gut level that affiliation has no room for conflict. On the other side of the equation, men are motivated by the need for respect. Conflict may well be a necessary ingredient in the accumulation of respect. Neither style of interaction or motivation is necessarily better or worse, healthier or sicker than the other; they are just different. Both men and women are tired of being told they are "wrong" for doing things the way they do them. As with establishing peerness, it is important to be able to accept differences. It is through an understanding and acceptance of differences that communication can be enhanced.

THE SPIRIT OF COMPETITION

America is a culture that is driven by competition; it is our number one obsession. The spirit of competition can be witnessed everywhere in the media and in our collective obsession with comparing ourselves with others, seeing if we measure up. Competition surrounds us in the form of commercial advertising, professional sports, and the mad dash up the corporate ladder. Our economic system is built on competition, and most of the business and professional world knows little else. We've institutionalized competition by convincing ourselves that it is an inherent part of being human. In his book *No Contest* Alfie Kohn makes an excellent argument against this assumption with which I tend to agree.[3] Competition, like comparison, is an invasion of our self-esteem and, as such, an invasion of personal boundaries.

Organized team sports serve to train children from a young age in the hierarchical power structure of the culture. Just as in the ordeal of waiting to be picked by one team or the other, children get a clear reading of their standing among classmates. For girls it is important to be popular, and for boys it is important to be the best. This basic difference obviously leads them to compete with differing energy and intention.

The spirit of competition compels us to beat other people because within competition someone has to lose in order for someone else to win. Here is the one-up, one-down problem that prevents peerness. Competition is supported and defended by four cultural myths: competition is an unavoidable fact of life; competition motivates us to do the best; contests are fun; and competition builds character. These four myths appear to be determined to shield the spirit of competition from scrutiny and the possibility of change. Furthermore, these principles blind us to the importance of cooperation. We are so frantically locked into the competitive struggle that we have forgotten the ease that cooperation can provide. The tyranny of the male style of conflict and status has overshadowed the female style of cooperation. The competitive hierarchy of our culture makes it hard to connect with other people. It is sealing off our interpersonal boundaries. Someone caught in the all-consuming clutches of fierce competition is unlikely to be connected with his own needs and feelings; he is too busy being a robot for the culture. It is impossible to connect and share with anyone who is not first connected to himself.

Dr. Tannen describes women's style of communication as being motivated by the desire for cooperation and connection. But within the male framework of this society, activities of sharing, cooperating, helping, and comforting are interpreted as less important than the male approach of challenging, strategizing, and winning. While competition interferes with communication, it remains the style that is rewarded and valued within our culture. People with the cooperative style can listen to and tolerate differing points of view, while competitive people seek to convince and persuade. When the people with whom we communicate become opponents, they become objects, and companionship and intimacy have only a small chance for survival. Competition, by its very nature, damages relationships between people. There may be camaraderie, but in any competition there has to be a winner and a loser, one up and one down. Peerness is not a possibility under the design of competition.

While it is true that women seek cooperation as a general rule, their relationship to competition is changing. As women have moved more and more into the workplace, they have increasingly adopted the attitudes and appearance of men. Popular magazines targeted at the professional woman show them in suits carrying briefcases, feminine versions of their male counterparts. One hopes that women will not totally embrace the aggressiveness of men, but they have certainly adopted the uniform.

Instead of encouraging and coaxing the unique and best qualities out of individuals, competition actually pounds us into conformity. When we have to look a certain way, drive a certain car, and have a certain lifestyle, we are unable to take risks and to generate our own standards. We have given up our unique outlooks and visions to the status-seeking status quo of the culture. We have opened our boundaries to definition by a culture into which we have little input. So when the culture encourages us to drink alcohol, work too hard, tell lies, drive too fast, take drugs, and live on the edge, we collude in our self-destruction.

Deep down, many of us carry a gnawing belief that we are not good enough. We think we have to prove ourselves constantly. We hate ourselves and believe that others do, too. We don't honor our basic humanity. We are driven to compete with others in our constant battle to prove something, to yank our self-esteem out of the mud. This is the result of spiritual boundary damage.

The winning-at-all-costs mentality has led us toward unhealthy life choices. In business it pushes people to work too hard for too many hours a day. Work can be an effective and lucrative distraction for anyone who doesn't have a private life or is trying to escape the one he does have. Winning creates tremendous pressure that encourages people to cheat, cut corners, and lie. We rationalize our cut corners, telling ourselves that other people are doing it all the time, so why shouldn't we. We accept behavior that is cruel, ruthless, even deceitful in the pursuit of winning.

Students are likewise driven by this competitive ideology. They stay up late, drink caffeine, maybe take stimulants, and smoke cigarettes in a studying ritual that is expected to produce the best grade.

Athletes push their bodies unmercifully, take steroids, follow demanding diets, and practice for many hours a day. They force their bodies to endure tremendous pain and discomfort for the sole purpose of not having to lose.

Strict competitive sports require an altered approach to the living of one's life that verges on abuse. Once a person, usually a child, makes a commitment to a sport, he is forced to narrow his experiences and behavior. He has less time for friends and other social interactions.

Developmentally he begins to fall behind. If he stays with the sport, his obsession with it must grow to meet the escalating demands of competition. He must submit to ruthless regimentation. Some people refer to this particular addiction as "jockaholism."

Indoctrination into our competitive culture begins earlier and earlier these days. Children can now enroll in readiness programs that will put them in a better position to get into the "best" kindergartens. Once they are in school, we teach their squirmy little bodies how to sit still, clap in rhythm, and march in stiff, straight lines. We train their minds to get the "right" answer. Imagination is molded and shaped to conform to the curriculum. Individuality is not rewarded; instead, we are taught the manners of the culture. Children learn quickly that making mistakes is not permitted under the spirit of competition. On any playground in America you can hear small children taunting one another, "Anything you can do, I can do better." We prime our children in school for the competition of the workplace. The whole concept of cooperation gets lost in the idea of obedience before the child reaches the fourth grade. Our culture brutally evaluates anything less than the "best." We concentrate on results to the exclusion of enjoying the process of working, playing, sharing, and learning. Furthermore, when we train children to be obedient, to not stand up for their rights, we rob them of the ability to protect and defend themselves. We sentence them to victimization.

We grade and rank children publicly in school. This same positioning goes on throughout life—the career track, the income level, the economic status, the professional standing, the class acceptance. We're always trying to get to the head of the pack. In this race we endure tension headaches, high blood pressure, anxiety, stress, and early death. Competition is damaging to our physical, spiritual, emotional, and social health. The more we compete, the more we need to compete. This is the very substance of addiction.

Ultimately, our drive to compete is born of low self-esteem and the belief that we can raise our self-worth by lowering someone else's. Competition cannot survive without comparison and is therefore self-destructive. Sufficient damage has been done to our sense of ourselves that we are constantly comparing ourselves and competing to prove that we are better, prettier, faster, smarter, or richer than someone else. Competition makes true sharing impossible. Sharing requires both sides to have healthy identities.

Couples engage in clandestine record keeping; they keep track of one another and pull out the tally sheets in the heat of an argument. Statements like "You always get to be the one who decides" and "Whenever I want to go out, you are always too tired. So no, I don't want to go to the movie" show that accounting is taking place and being mentally recorded. Instead of discussing differences and the possible need for adjustment or compromise, such couples are hoarding disappointments to be used as weapons in future battles. Again, this is not a very useful behavior in the promotion of healthy communication.

Ideally, human beings grow up believing that the world is a safe place where their needs will be met. But when the world is construed as a rat race and competition abounds, this innate sense of security gets damaged by anxiety and a loss of trust. Violence is done to spiritual, mental, and intellectual boundaries when trust and security are impaired. When people are pitted against one another competitively, there is little chance for genuine sharing.

THE DEPRIVED MIND

Scarcity means that there isn't enough of something to go around. For those of us with damaged self-esteem it often feels that there isn't enough of anything good to go around, and surely when it does come around, we will be at the end of the line. People with this outlook live in a psychological state of chronic deprivation. Anything good that happens to other people is perceived as a loss. Having one's needs met seems unquestionably hopeless. The definition of one's boundary is extremely weak. John described his feelings this way:

It's like I think there's someone out there who has it in for me. They're out there watching and making sure that nothing good is going to come my way. And if something happens to get by, and something good happens, I'm just waiting for him to figure it out and snatch it back. The worst part is that if something good happens for someone else, instead of feeling happy for them, I feel like I lost out. I just never feel like I've got my share.

Poor self-esteem is a major contributor to most psychological problems and self-injurious thoughts and behaviors. Our beliefs about ourselves and the world are tied up with our self-esteem. It is our beliefs that inform our choices and guide our attention. Our beliefs can lead us to justify the improper actions of others toward us and the damaging acts we perpetrate on ourselves. This all goes back to the period of childhood when we learned either that the world was a safe and nurturing place where our needs would be met consistently and on time or that the world was a harsh and punitive place where our needs would be met with abuse and neglect. Experiences at this stage of development may leave us dependent, wanting and waiting for our physical, intellectual, spiritual, and emotional needs to be met by someone or something outside ourselves.

People with such a flimsy sense of self look to others for definition. They do not have a healthy sense of personal boundaries. We violate everyone's boundaries by trying to please everyone. Overinvolved people are more afraid of hurting others than of being hurt. In the process of taking care of others they damage themselves by doing too much. At the same time they send a message to others that they are the experts and have greater competence. They flip back and forth between the narcissistic high of having anticipated and fulfilled someone's needs and the depressed low of chronic deprivation and feeling used by others. This style of relating is not honest sharing and is not conducive to establishing a peer relationship.

On the flip side of this style of boundary violator are the people who shut down, close the borders, slam all the doors when they feel that someone has hurt them. They seal their anger inside, never letting the words of their feelings be heard. At the same time they refuse to interact with the person they feel has harmed them. They punish by withdrawing affection and attention. Consciously or not, these people expect their minds to be read and their actions to be interpreted as a cry for amends and apologies. They are often unsatisfied with the results of their manipulations. They are cooped up with their rage in self-imposed isolation. This style of relating is not honest sharing.

Some people use seduction as a means of gaining attention, raising their self-esteem, and making a connection with another human being. These people will accept attention, touching, and sex that they may not truly want but are unable to refuse. They may not be assertive enough to resist the advances of another person, or they ignore their reservations for the sake of a high they get from connecting. Sexuality is used to manipulate other people and to provide a fleeting sense of well-being. Poor self-esteem has convinced these people that they have little else to offer. Their sense of well-being depends on their attractiveness and desirability to another person. In the extreme cases of sexual addiction, sexuality becomes compulsive, abusive, and even dangerous. This style of relating is unhealthy sharing.

People who are overachievers, who are rigid, and who constantly think in terms of absolute right and wrong also suffer from severe deficits in self-esteem. They look to perfectionistic outcomes to prove their worth. They seek approval through respect and praise from others, never thinking that it might be found within themselves. These people may present a self-righteous front to cover up their high levels of fear and insecurity. Or they may be filled with rage, always in a fury over something, desperately trying to create a shred of self-worth with their bravado. These deprived individuals often mouth the sentiments of racism, sexism, homophobia, and intolerance with the loudest voice.

When we are rigid, we are trapped by absolutes. Everything is seen through the narrow lens of right and wrong, good and bad, black and white, and the range of our vision is severly constricted. We believe that our resources are scant. It is through actively changing our belief in limited resources that we begin to achieve some flexibility. As children we might have gotten the idea that a person can feel only one emotion at a time and learned that certain experiences produce certain feelings. We did not learn that in any particular situation we could feel either fear or excitement or both. Back then there were no choices. Our feelings were programmed early, then they slipped down below the level of our awareness.

Religious zealotry can be an avenue for escaping self-confrontation and covering up a faltering sense of self. Zealots' poor self-esteem gets soothed by their absorption in religious practices and beliefs. These people try to convince you to love the Lord as they do. They trespass on your intellectual and spiritual boundaries.

I do not wish to suggest that all religious practice is dangerous and intrusive—far from it. But there comes a point when religion becomes condemning of diversity, rigid in its outlook, and invasive in its approach. This is what I call religious zealotry, and it is not indicative of healthy sharing.

Addiction is the ultimate way to avoid intimacy and

connection with the self and others. In addiction the person has a primary relationship with a substance or a behavior that precludes any others. Addiction makes honest sharing impossible. Addiction often begins as a misguided attempt to soothe feelings of low self-esteem. The gambler gets a shot of good feelings when he wins. The woman takes great pride in the cleanliness of her home. The office manager feels relaxed as she sips her third martini. The shrewd businessman pats himself on the back for beating out the little guys. The anorexic feels superior because she ate only six hundred calories all day. However, it is the curse of addiction that these false "highs" are short-lived and eventually require more of the drug of choice to produce the desired effects. Addiction drags us down, devastates us psychologically and physically, ruins our relationships, and interferes with our performance. These are certainly not desirable outcomes for someone needing to bolster his self-esteem.

In a competitive culture we organize and give meaning to our lives by aquiring things: money, toys, status. The compulsion to accumulate things acts as a substitute for whatever is lacking in our souls. We soothe the pain of a deprived childhood with an adulthood filled with consumption. There is a big hole in our soul into which we shove big houses, fancy cars, jewelry, VCRs, and whatever else we think will ease the pain. We repress fears of not being liked by buying lavish presents for people. To stay ahead of loneliness and self-doubt we keep struggling up the corporate ladder, or the social ladder, or the political ladder. We have no understanding of what *enough* is.

In short, when we look outside ourselves for what is lacking inside, we are looking in the wrong place. As long as we ignore or remain oblivious to our inner selves, we will continue to cause ourselves harm. It is time that the concept of self-centeredness lost its extremely negative connotation.

"EXCUSE ME, EXCUSE ME"

A seven-year-old child walks into the room where her mother and I are talking. She says, "Excuse me," and launches into the question she has come to ask.

Her mother reprimands her. "Don't interrupt us."

"But I said 'Excuse me,'" cries the eager and defeated daughter.

"Well, yes, you did, but you don't just come into a room and say 'Excuse me' and expect everyone to be quiet and listen to you. You have to wait for an opening."

"Well, I just wanted to know if I can go over to Jerry's house to play."

Children don't have much of a concept of conversational openings and the effects of interruption. They do not intend to violate anyone else's right to speak; they are merely trying to get some information or state a fact. Their needs are immediate, they are impulsive, and they speak as soon as they have a thought.

Between adults, however, interrupting can be perceived as a hostile act of bullying, not paying attention, disinterest, or an attempt to dominate the conversation. People who habitually need to dominate conversations, who interrupt and talk over other speakers, are probably performing for the purpose of gaining attention from others. These are the people who seem to be constantly onstage. They tell funny jokes and stories, or they are experts who know something about everything. They appear comfortable with themselves, but as a friend wisely advised me once, don't judge people's insides by their outsides. Such extroverts may be the life of the party, but they can also be rude and insensitive. It is hard to connect and maintain intimacy with someone who does not listen, someone who only talks.

Asking questions can be another form of interruption. To one person a question inserted into the middle of a conversation can be perceived as a need for clarification. Another person may construe it as an intrusion, being thrown off his train of thought. I first noticed these differences at professional conferences. Sometimes a participant will throw out a question in the middle of a lecture. Some of the lecturers will stop, shift gears, and answer the question. Other speakers appear irritated with the interruption and answer that they will come back to the question when they are finished with the prepared talk.

Interruption is a matter of individual perception. Whether questioning is perceived as an interruption or merely a question depends on the extent to which a person feels compelled to answer. He may decide to get back to it in time. Therefore, he does not experience the question as an interruption. A person can feel interrupted even if the other person did not intend to interrupt. The concept of interruption is important in the understanding of communication. The basic intention for men in communication is not always the same as it is for women. This fact is the cause of much misunderstanding and miscommunication between the sexes.

There is a vast difference between the styles in which men and women approach the issues of apology and blame. There is plenty of status wrapped around each. For men an apology lowers status; it implies fault and blame. Men are loath to be in the one-down position of having done something wrong, and as a result some men rarely apologize. On the other hand, women see apology as a means of expressing concern or mending fences.

I think both men and women respond to real or imagined blame more than is necessary, especially those of us who were shamed as children or parented by guilt. These individuals carry such a storehouse of guilt that they imagine blame where it does not exist. Some people respond passively with an apology. These are the people who are constantly saying "I'm sorry" or "I know this is a stupid question and you probably don't want to answer it, but . . ." Then there are the people who respond to their internalized guilt aggressively. They are so desperate to escape their feelings of guilt and shame that they confront the world with a harsh exterior. These are the people who oppose authority and take no responsibility for their actions if they are caught. They accuse others of incompetence and accuse equipment of malfunctioning rather than accepting the consequences of their transgressions.

Women and men are often frustrated with one another in relationships because of what is interpreted by either gender as implied blame or apparent lack of concern. Because we are unaware of the underlying differences in motivation between men and women, we draw conclusions about behavior that are based solely on our own point of view. The inevitable subtle disappointment hampers our work toward sharing.

PUSH-ME, PULL-ME FRIENDS

I know many men and women who find it difficult to open up and share with another human being because their privacy was violated during childhood. Maybe they had intrusive mothers who read their mail or their diaries. Or maybe their fathers assigned motives to every behavior or desire: "Oh, I know why you want to do that; you just want all the other boys to think you are the toughest." Kids who are sentenced to grow up with invasive parents have a hard time when they reach adolescence. It is during the period of adolescence when a child struggles with issues of autonomy and identity. It is a time when he needs some privacy. Children who don't get this sort of privacy believe that getting to know other people is a requirement—not a choice. Such a belief will cause them to rush into friendships or shy away from the possibility.

An enmeshed family is an invasive family where privacy and autonomy are not repected or preserved. The confidence and self-esteem of family members are sacrificed within these families. When enmeshment is the model of interaction you are familiar with, you tend to fashion friendships and romantic relationships in the same manner. You rush into intimacy because not being close to another individual makes you feel uneasy. You want to know everything there is to know about someone right away and want to be together constantly. You fall in love with anyone who reaches out, maybe even with those who don't. Sometimes you find that other people back away from you, saying things like "You're too intense" and "Not so fast; I'm not ready for this."

However, if enmeshment was your family's style of interaction but you hated it, you may approach people believing that if you let them come anywhere near you, they will crawl right under your skin and engulf you. You read signals very carefully. If someone seems too eager, you are gone. You are distrustful of the intentions of other people and tend to hold yourself in reserve. Sometimes you are so distant that you lose any sense of connection to humanity at all. Basically you don't feel very safe with people. People say things to you like "You're so cold" and "Gee, you sure are hard to get to know."

People have vastly different needs for personal space and interaction with others. Some people feel deprived if they don't have a dinner date four nights a week. They can't stand to be alone in a room that doesn't have some noise in it. For others the thought of going to even one party a year causes them to think about crawling into a shell. They love long periods of quiet, alone time. How an individual develops his style of being depends on his personality characteristics and experiences throughout life. No style should be judged right or wrong, good or bad. Styles are just different. Accepting differences and not holding back feelings are two important elements in honest communication. They are crucial ingredients for improved sharing.

Problems can arise in communication when two people have widely opposed styles of approach and withdrawal. The sad irony is that many people are attracted to the type that is most dissimilar to their own. Obviously this makes for some differences and difficulties in attachment and separation needs. One partner may be feeling crowded while the other is feeling abandoned by the same interaction. If these partners cannot talk honestly about their feelings and work out some sort of compromise, one or both will be forced to repress feelings and begin storing resentment.

I am someone who demands greater amounts of quiet, alone time than most people do. My nerves are frayed by parties. I like to have conversations with one or two people at a time; mingling is not one of my skills. If I am allowed to exercise my preferences, I will generally opt to be alone or with a small group of intimate friends. I am attracted, however, to extroverts, people who appear comfortable with other people, who can tell jokes and entertain in social situations.

Over the years I have found that these people and I have a tendency to play push-me, pull-me with one another in terms of communication. One will approach, the other will retreat, and vice versa. It is difficult to respond to someone's request for personal space without feeling a twinge of rejection. This is another personal boundary issue. If we are secure within ourselves and our well-being is not being determined by the actions of another person, then a simple request for space can be received as just that, a request, not a demand and not a rejection. The same thing is true when one partner approaches and wishes more contact. The responses are still the same—yes and no. But as we have seen, because we have come to believe that "No" means "I don't like you," we have sacrificed that option. Until two individuals can have boundaries healthy enough that their self-esteem is not dependent on someone else, they are destined to remain among the sharing-imparied.

A few years ago I had the opportunity to visit China. We traveled to many different parts of the country, but the day I will never forget was when we took a bus from Luoyang to Yangzhou. For six hours we drove through a sea of people. The bus driver honked the horn the entire trip. I remember thinking that eventually we would reach the end of town and the crowd would thin out until we got to the outskirts of the next town. Well, there were no outskirts, just people, thousands and thousands of people. I felt very anxious after a few hours, and claustrophobic. I kept asking myself over and over, Where do these people go to be alone? The thought that the answer might be "nowhere" filled me with terror. Not to be able to go somewhere and be alone with oneself and one's thoughts was a horrifying thought to someone who has the luxury to do so with regularity.

There are, I am sure, people who are stimulated and energized by huge crowds of people. For them the idea of a weekend at home with nothing to do but relax fills then with the same terror I experienced in China. For friends, lovers, and spouses, learning to honestly negotiate differing needs for closeness and withdrawal will ultimately enhance sharing.

Communication is a tricky thing, especially with those we love the most. When a healthy system of communication is in operation, information flows. What is put out has something to do with what is received, and what is received has something to do with what is sent out later. It is an interactive system capable of changes and modifications depending on the information that is passing in and out.

When each side in the communication process has set limits and boundaries and when those boundaries are respected by both sides, then the system can work to transmit both positive and negative messages in either direction. Without boundaries, neither side has adequate protection and communication suffers.

Projecting our feelings out onto other people is not a healthy style of communication. When we assign feelings to others, we are not taking responsibility for ourselves. We are giving our feelings to someone else and then convincing ourselves that we did not.

Maggie Scarf, in her book *Intimate Partners*, states that one of the major problems in close, committed relationships is that partners cannot distinguish between what is going on inside one's own head and what is going on inside the head of one's partner.[4] This is most certainly an issue of insufficient personal boundaries.

Has anyone ever said to you, "I feel you are angry at me"? There is the possibility that you *were* angry without actually knowing it, and this query might have helped clarify your feelings. But there is another possibility. The other person may be feeling anger, but rather than acknowledge it, he projects the feeling onto you. If this is the case, your response to "I feel you are angry at me" may be that you have been incorrectly described. Your emotional boundary has been intruded on.

"I feel you are angry at me" is often indirect and dishonest communication. It starts out as a statement of the speaker's feelings, but in the middle it shifts to a description of the other person's feelings. Tricky. The receiver of this message must respond to the imposition of a feeling he may not actually have. He has been labeled. Yet he knows nothing about why the other person feels the way he does.

Some would argue that it's merely a matter of semantics, but there is a different emotional climate and a different quality of sharing generated by "I feel you are angry at me" versus "I'm feeling anxious, and I'm wondering, are you angry at me?" This is a tricky and critical difference for the sharing-impaired to grasp.

DID YOU HEAR?

Gossip is defined as the sharing of intimate fact with a third party. This is a simple enough definition to which the culture has added shades of good and bad, juicy and dull, hot and troublesome. While there may be some sense of taboo surrounding gossip, we send reporters into celebrities' garbage cans to hunt for information that can be printed in the tabloids. The tabloids are then bought weekly by millions of readers. For anyone in the public eye the boundary between public and private has been torn away. Slogans like "Inquiring minds want to know" speak of our collective hunger for gossip. The media creates programs like "Lifestyles of the Rich and Famous" so that we can passively and vicariously slip into the bedrooms, swimming pools, and vacations of complete strangers.

In some respects gossip has become like any other addiction: We know we shouldn't do it, but we can't help ourselves. I actually have a friend who is actively involved in recovery from her addiction to *People* magazine. It may sound funny, but she recognized she had a dependency for the weekly magazine and decided to try to curb her urge. She is managing to stay "sober," but the last time we spoke she admitted, "I really had a hard time passing by the one with Oprah on the cover saying she would never diet again."

The addiction to gossip seems to me to be another way of avoiding being present with ourselves. It is a way to step outside ourselves and intrude on the privacy of others. Gossip is a way to escape and slip into the true or falsified world of someone else. The same can be said of soap operas (and I must admit that I love them myself). They are an escape, a way to forget one's own troubles and concerns while being engrossed in the bigger and more dramatic troubles of the characters.

There is nothing inherently wrong with escape and fantasy. When it becomes compulsive, we need to be concerned: when we would rather watch "All My Children" than get a job or rather read the *Star* than meet a friend for dinner. Another danger lies in developing what seems like a relationship with soap opera stars or our favorite tabloid queens and kings. I have overheard conversations in which people were discussing TV characters as if they were friends, not actors and actresses performing. In the extreme, an addiction to gossip can take the place of any other intimate sharing. I think some people opt for relationships with unresponsive images instead of having a true, intimate, and sharing relationship with people.

There is also the sort of gossip that is shared among people who actually know one another. The intimate details of health, well-being, finances, romances, and the ups and downs of daily life are exchanged. Dr. Tannen oberves that men and women approach the issue of gossip from their characteristically different styles of communication. Women share intimate details as a way to feel close, to cement friendships. Men may feel betrayed or uneasy upon hearing the details of their personal lives being discussed. A woman sees gossip as *talk about*, while a man views it as *talk against*.

Throughout this chapter we have taken a look at the behaviors, postures, and cultural directives that influence honest sharing and communication between people. There is much that adversely affects people's ability to connect with one another. Everyone brings his own personal history, damaged boundaries, and fears into every interaction. It is through the examination of differences in style, motivation, intention, and outcome of sharing that we can gain understanding and a broader range of alternatives for ourselves. With these new and expanded options we can soften barriers and extend boundaries. We can begin to feel safer and more secure in a bigger world. We can connect with a greater community rather than staying isolated and frightened.

The following are some clear examples of harmful patterns of communication that can develop in any relationship and cause it to be categorized among the sharing-impaired:

Nagging
Abusive criticism
Accepting mistreatment
Possessiveness
Living one's life through the other person
Demanding that your friend or partner live up to your
    standards
Avoiding responsibility through passivity
Using sex as a reward or punishment
Picking fights to prove your love
Picking fights to feel connected
Having to have the last word
Competitiveness
Interrupting
Holding back feelings (this is the same as lying)
Expecting total satisfaction from others

CHAPTER 5

Does the Noise Inside My Head Bother You?

$\mathcal{T}$HE LAST CHAPTER COVERED INTERPERSONAL COMMUNI-
cation; this one is concerned with communication with
the self. In *Little Miss Perfect* I talked quite a bit about
internal dialogue and watching how and what we say to
ourselves. I have such a loud and active internal dialogue that sometimes I imagine that other people will be
able to overhear me! Therefore, I named this chapter after a phrase used to describe enmeshed family systems.

Sometimes I think of internal dialogue in the same
way I would think of an enmeshed family. There are
voices that intrude, finish sentences, and have very poor
senses of boundary. Internal dialogue is literally the

voices of our thoughts, and as such, it can be terribly distracting. I have had two assistants while working on this book, and I've named them Manic Voice and Depressive Voice. Depressive Voice informs me at regular intervals that I don't know what I am doing or where I am going with this book. She assures me that I will not have enough material to complete the project. Fortunately, I have an antidote, Manic Voice, who is filled with praise and wonder over the vision and surprise of this book. She sees the big picture and assures me that everything is going along all right. She also knows when I need to step back and do something else for a few days. These two voices have been a tremendous help. Despite the difference messages, they have been able to keep me focused. They have been part of my support system.

Our internal dialogue—what we say to ourselves and how we say it—is a prime indicator of the state of our self-esteem. Through research I have come to believe that there are people for whom an internal dialogue has been completely silenced or at least grossly distorted.

Alice Miller, who is probably the most outspoken opponent of child abuse and a forceful advocate for children, writes:

> The only possible recourse a baby has when his screams are ignored is to repress the distress, which is tantamount to mutilating his soul, for the result is an interference with his ability to feel, to be aware, and to remember.[1]

I suspect this child's inner voice is either quiet or telling lies.

Repression is the only way an infant can deal with feelings and desires that are either punished or ignored by his parents. The child desperately wants not to lose the closeness, love, and nurturance of the caretaker and will damage his inner self to secure those things. This is the beginning stage at which subsequent self-destructive or abusive behavior takes hold. Remember, anything we repress eventually becomes an obsession. Alice Miller argues that repression and abuse are a gift that keeps on giving. When we hide from ourselves the truth of what happened in our childhoods, we are doomed to repeat them in our lives and with our children. The cycle of child abuse cannot stop without the realization and healing of suppressed wounds. Contrary to public sentiment, Miller demands that we shed the cultural conspiracy of protecting and urging forgiveness for abusive parents and begin holding them responsible for their actions. She writes: "Not to take one's suffering seriously, to make light of it or even to laugh at it, is considered good manners in our culture."[2]

Throughout the writing of this book there has been a nagging voice inside me that says, "You are being too harsh on parents; they don't mean to do this stuff. They do the best they can." Well, Alice Miller must not have that same voice inside her head. While she recognizes that parents abuse their children because of repressed feelings from their own childhoods, she says it is up to adults to rout their repressed sufferings and get whatever help is necessary to heal themselves. In this way, the suffering is not passed on to the next generation.

She argues that our collective reluctance to blame parents and hold them accountable reinforces the status quo and allows children to continue being abused. Incidentally, the exact words of my internal admonisher were actually spoken to me when I was a child by a woman who took care of me. When I was hurt or angry, she would hold me and let me cry, all the while chanting the words "It's all right, honey. Your parents love you; they are doing the best they know how." I got the training of the culture directly from her, and I took it in along with her loving embrace.

Have you ever told a story from your childhood as if it had happened to someone else? This is one of the ways we remove ourselves from our feelings and silence the child within us who was hurt. This sort of detachment will leave memories intact but will remove our feelings to the extent that we are safe from their surprise attack. This safety net has a big price tag. When we don't feel pain, we can't know when something is wrong and can't protect ourselves.

I know a woman who retells clearly abusive incidences from her childhood as if she were telling a joke. She smiles and always makes the stories entertaining. There is never the slightest glimmer of sadness or pain for the little girl in those stories. When I have asked her if she is troubled by those events now, from her adult perspective, seeing herself as a child to whom they are happening, her answer is always a resounding "No, of course not." She has insulated and removed herself so completely from the experience of that child that she might as well have killed her. There is little doubt that this kind of self-protection is ultimately self-destructive.

According to Alice Miller and many others, such unresolved trauma will absolutely destine this woman to act out her repressed childhood suffering and rage. She may engage in any variety of self-destructive behavior in order to keep her feelings in check, or she may vent her pent-up rage on her children. This is one explanation why so many abused children grow up to be abusers. It is also the reason why ninety percent of all the violent criminals in jail were abused children. I suspect the other ten percent are lying or cannot remember.

Some children who are exposed to trauma and forced to withstand horrifying experiences will shut down to the extent that their memories are erased completely. Not only the feelings have been repressed, but the actual memory as well. This ability to forget is often found in survivors of sexual abuse for whom the trauma was so great that the only way they could cope was to believe that it had never happened at all. This explains why so many survivors are not aware that they were abused.

Healing from the damage and abuse we suffered as small children requires reestablishing some sort of internal dialogue with a child who is scared and hurt. It is through the healing of this child and our ability to be in free conversation with our lost self that we begin to use the phrases in Chapter 3 or create our own to set limits and boundaries for ourselves. It is this voice that must heal by learning how to say "No."

I GOT THE BLUES SO BAD ONE TIME IT PUT MY FACE IN A PERMANENT FROWN[3]

Depression is an emotional state characterized by sadness, self-doubt, and a lack of interest in people and the events of daily life. People suffering from depression have poor self-images, cannot experience happiness or optimism, and feel hopeless and unable to generate alternatives for themselves. Depressed people feel stuck in their gloom.

Endogenous depression is depression that arises within an individual without any apparent external stimulus or life situation to cause it. For some this sort of depression has its root cause in biochemistry. For many others the causes are psychological, stemming from negative childhood experiences that have in all likelihood been repressed or forgotten. The inability to express real feelings, particularly aggressive ones, in a normal way leads to depression. People without "No" are frequently depressed.

Symptoms of depression include agitation or lack of energy, pessimism, self-blame and self-criticism, passivity, and feelings of guilt, sadness, anger, loneliness, lack of interest, and low self-worth. A person with this diminished state of being is not capable of maintaining or protecting healthy boundaries. A depressed person is vulnerable to abuse from others as well as from himself.

Depression is a form of punishment. It is a way to keep our feelings pressed down and out of the way. In the process it functions like any other addiction. For those for whom depression has become a chronic state, there is no alternative. They have forgotten, if they ever knew, that there are ways of feeling other than depression.

The internal climate for depressed people sends messages that convince them that they are being punished for the guilt they feel over not attaining something. These people constantly replay situations in their minds, looking for their fault, their stupidity, their inadequacy. I used to wake up with a jolt in the middle of the night, tortured by this very behavior. I would revisit various social situations, review them, and start telling myself what I should and shouldn't have said. People who are tortured by constant internal criticism or carry the heavy weight of punitive religious dogma are likely to experience this sort of depression.

Anticipation and excessive and inappropriate worrying are other ways we punish ourselves. Depressed people may believe that anticipating disaster is prudent or that being anxious over an upcoming event is just a practical rehearsal. The fact is that these obsessive thoughts destroy pleasure and happiness and yank the person out of the present moment and scatter him fearfully between past and future. The behavior is constricting and depleting, but most of all it is completely useless. No disaster was ever averted because someone worried about it beforehand.

Depression is sustained through a constant internal litany of self-derision. Depressed people hound themselves, constantly put themselves down, cannot accept compliments from others, and depreciate and demean themselves with little or no awareness of the self-destructive consequences. Once again, without awareness there is no hope of change. Listen to yourself. If you make a mistake, what do you say to yourself? Depressed people berate themselves and give up, while healthier people perhaps even laugh at themselves while learning a lesson.

People who feel compelled to give lengthy explanations for themselves are often suffering from some degree of depression—the person who is ten minutes late for an appointment and spends the next ten explaining why, the person who lies to justify not being able to meet some request: "Oh, I wish I could go to that movie, but I have an appointment with my dentist that afternoon." These people do not have enough of a sense of self to believe that their wishes and needs can be met and respected.

Tremendous personal energy is consumed by depression. It is not easy to keep hidden from the self and others all of our constructive and creative aspects. Self-effacement is a full-time job. People suffering from depression look tired; they look like they are carrying a heavy load, and they are.

SCREAMING IN THE DARK

Self-hatred is exhibited by people whose internal world feels like a hostile territory. These people fiendishly use information only they possess to produce anxiety and fear within themselves. They know where their vulnerabilities lie, and they attack themselves unmercifully with disturbing and obsessive thoughts, panic attacks, hypochondria, and phobias. Maybe they have nightmares or disturbing daytime thoughts. Whatever the form, these people are experiencing an internal reign of terror.

Panic is actually caused by our own emotions; it happens when our feelings start to well up and scare us. Panic is what we feel because we fear being overwhelmed or harmed by feelings. Sometimes a painful memory from childhood emerges into our awareness, and we panic. Even though panic may appear to have no trigger, it is the feelings and memories we have repressed and forgotten that call panic to the rescue. Inside, there is a scared, shamed, or abused child who remembers everything, and panic is a way to keep him quiet, to prevent connections from being made, to obscure our awareness. Panic prevents us from knowing. The physiological changes associated with panic—rapid heartbeat and shortness of breath—can actually distort normal vision.

Panic feeds on itself. Unconsciously we get scared, we panic, we feel frightened and think we have to escape the feelings. We escalate the fear. While nothing about panic appears deliberate, it is actually an intentional reaction to the emergence of intolerable emotions and memories. It is an emotional distraction. Panic blocks our conscious awareness and, as such, is an act of self-hatred. Panic attacks are often found in conjunction with agoraphobia.

Attacks of hypochondria resemble panic attacks in that they provide a diversion, a shifting of attention, an obliteration of awareness. Becoming obsessive about our physical condition leaves little attention available for our emotions. Again, fear takes hold and becomes the only emotion that can be felt. Worst possible scenarios are imagined, dire results are expected, and in extreme cases physical symptoms can be manifested. Hypochondriacs, rather than facing their fears, project them onto their state of health.

Individuals who are compulsively driven by a fearful internal dialogue that convinces them of catastrophic physical ailments turn to doctors and healers for remedies for their fears and insecurity. The result: The true ailment is ignored, when the practitioner tries to convince the patient there is nothing wrong. Medicine that is not necessary may be dispensed, and in the worst cases people submit to unnecessary surgery. These "false remedies" put individuals at risk.

Related to hypochondria is a disorder called dysmorphophobia. In this case a person is obsessed with some unsatisfactory aspect of her face or body. She will spend excessive amounts of time ruminating on the imagined catastrophe of her imperfection. The women with anorexia nervosa discussed in Chapter 2 provide excellent examples of this disorder. Their internal dialogue about how their bodies look is completely out of sync with the actuality. Some anorexics actually starve to death thinking they are overweight.

Countless other imaginary blemishes can lead women into costly and dangerous plastic surgeries. I have already mentioned how the culture helps promote this particular form of self-hatred by reflecting desirable physical images that are unattainable by most humans.

I had a friend in school who had a perfectly normal and attractive face. All her features were perfectly normal and in balance with one another. She, however, was convinced that she had the largest, ugliest nose in the world. She spent hours looking at it, complaining about it, and trying to disguise it with makeup. Her poor nose took such verbal abuse; she hated it and never missed a chance to tell someone. At age sixteen she had a plan that she would have plastic surgery to get rid of the ugly thing. I lost contact with her before we turned sixteen, but I have little doubt that she followed through with that plan. I have often wondered what sort of thing she had "stuck her nose into" to be shamed into hating part of herself so completely.

WHOOPS!

There are some more subtle ways in which we create an internal environment that is self-punishing and prevents our true feelings from ever coming to our awareness. These tactics are so sneaky that people may not even notice them or may think they are just a normal part of everyday life. These self-destructive tactics can easily be rationalized away as common, everyday household accidents.

Some people seem to have more accidents than the norm. Maybe they burn themselves while cooking, fall off a ladder, slip on a wet floor—normal things that happen. But for these people they happen quite often. The accidents are more regular than they are serious. These people describe themselves as "clumsy" or "a big klutz" without ever stopping to wonder why.

Then there are the people who take more than the average amount of risk. They drive cars faster than the speed limit. When the traffic light turns yellow, they jam the gas pedal to the floor. They swim out too far in the ocean. Maybe they skydive, an activity that looks like a sport but actually involves great risk. People who have highly dangerous or superstressful jobs might also be suspected of having internal climates where it is hard to live. It appears that for some, living on the edge is preferable to living on the inside.

Certain physical ailments may have their primary stimulus in a person's emotional climate. High blood pressure, chronic pain, asthma, boils, hives, and rashes may all have emotional triggers. Traumas from childhood, many of which we have been able to consciously obliterate, remain stored in the body. Over the years those traumas can manifest themselves as various ailments and pain.

I believe a metaphor can be found in many forms of physical distress. One summer during my childhood I was sent away to summer camp. Despite all the activities and diversions, I was anxious and sad for most of the summer—a fact I was desperately trying not to feel or reveal to anyone else. Instead of honestly crying and feeling my pain, I kept it all locked up inside my body. My body manifested this pain as a series of sties. One after another welled up around my eyes, sometimes two at a time, for the entire eight weeks of camp. I had never had a sty before, and I have never had one since. No other campers were afflicted.

When the summer ended and I went home, my parents announced their plans to divorce. With that news, the tears that had been infecting my eyelids began to fall.

Admittedly, accidents, activities, and physical health can be argued to have nothing to do with repressed emotions. But as we are trying to find what we have hidden, everything deserves consideration. Human beings have an unbelievable ability to forget, disguise, deny, and otherwise remain unaware of almost anything. As children, when we were not allowed to see something as it actually was, we had no choice but to overlook or disguise our perceptions. Our reality became foggy, and we learned the survival tactic of blurring our attention.

Our belief system is a major contributor to our internal dialogue. Treasured illusions about what constitutes happiness and how to achieve it can ultimately destroy any possibility for happiness at all. People with damaged boundaries believe that happiness comes from the outside—more money, the hottest car, a promotion, a new lover, a big win at the races, a new jewel, a drink.

The culture constantly promotes the myth that money is happiness. The message is blaring everywhere that power and possessions cure all ills. While it is possible that scheming, working, and acquiring can keep us busy and artificially boost our self-esteem, happiness is an illusion when it is applied from the outside. This materialistic tactic is symptomatic of a damaged boundary system. The disguises of happiness distract us from our true selves and our feelings. Money and its trappings are just another way to neglect ourselves, though it looks quite the opposite. For people who house a sad, lonely, longing child inside, there is nothing that can be acquired that will satisfy. That child is locked inside, and we are applying a remedy from the outside.

Accomplishment and fame are another false remedy

for sagging self-esteem. We think we will accept ourselves finally if enough other people do. We push ourselves toward excellence at the expense of fun and relaxation, telling ourselves that achievement is the only worthwhile outcome of our behavior. Guilt ensues whenever we deviate from our strict schedules and career paths. We silence the child inside who just wants to play. It is significant that there are high levels of drug and alcohol abuse and suicide among the "successful" segments of society.

Beauty and popularity also push us into self-destructive acts and activities solely for the sake of conformity. Everyone wants to fit in with some group, to belong and be popular. If our internal dialogue urges us to do anything to conform, we may find ourselves taking drugs and sneaking cigarettes in the school bathroom, piercing countless holes in our earlobes, putting chemicals on our hair, wearing girdles or spike-heeled shoes, getting tattoos, having liposuction, or getting silicone breast implants or a hair transplant. We go to great lengths to become what the culture defines as beautiful because our internal dialogue tells us we are ugly and unacceptable.

Some would argue that there is nothing inherently wrong with any of the choices people make to improve their looks and acceptability. I would argue that because the idea for these choices comes from outside the person's psyche, they are not in the person's true self-interest. I have actually heard about support groups for women who describe themselves as addicted to plastic surgery. They take the repeated risk of anesthesia and complications to compulsively construct what they hope to be the perfect face or body. I recently saw part of a talk show where women were speaking out about the horrible consequences that resulted when their breast implants migrated or ruptured inside their bodies. It was so frightening, I could watch for only a few minutes.

Through the process of hearing and understanding our internal dialogue we gradually become aware of our self-intent. We begin to recognize when we are hurting ourselves and when we truly have our own best interests at heart. It is from the position of caring for ourselves that we begin to construct and maintain healthy personal boundaries. As long as we are denying and repressing memories, ignoring the pain from our past, and projecting the popular culture's values, we will never be able to make choices that are for our own good.

A FRIENDLY VOICE

Many different internal dialogue processes have been discussed. None is desirable, though some may provide a false sense of safety. Most of us are probably uncomfortably familiar with one or more of these styles. If these are the ramblings and ruminations of an unhealthy mind, what would a healthy mind tell us?

Many of the obsessive thoughts we carry around in our minds keep our attention focused on the past or the future. It is too frightening to live in the present. In the present we run the risk of experiencing the feelings that we work so hard to keep at bay. In the present we have to *be* present. So, in a misguided attempt to protect ourselves, we distract ourselves from our present, sort of like living in an emotional twilight zone. Most of us experience ourselves as being in the moment, when in fact we are living emotionally in another time altogether. In the healing process of learning to live fully in the present it is crucial that we become able to ascertain where our attention is focused. Wherever our attention is focused is where we are headed. But this does not necessarily mean that if our attention is focused on the future, we are moving forward. Therefore, it is important to be able to locate our focus, to figure out exactly where it is that our attention lies.

The next step involves being able to adjust the focus of our attention back to the present moment whenever that becomes necessary. This process will be discussed in greater detail later in this book. Once we can honestly and consistently live in the present moment, we will speak to ourselves with greater care and be able to establish and maintain the limits and boundaries of our choosing with ourselves and other people. A healthy mind lives in the present and keeps its internal dialogue focused there as well. This is not to say that the past and the future do not influence us, only that there are distinct differences in our experience depending on where we turn our attention. When we live in the present moment, extraneous events are not able to provide the same distractions and other people cannot knock us off our center. In the present we can consistently maintain the self-center.

In Chapter 4 I suggested that it is high time for the concept of self-centeredness to lose its negative connotation. Traditionally we have defined self-centered behavior as arrogant, uncaring, and irresponsible. We have labeled people who are self-centered as selfish, thoughtless, and disrespectful. I am suggesting that we change how we use the term. Instead of a negative connotation, *self-centered* can come to mean inner-focused, taking responsibility for the self, and fully in touch with and honoring our true feelings. I think we need to use the descriptors *arrogant*, *selfish*, *irresponsible*, and the like to describe those specific attributes in people and reserve *self-centered* as a positive affirmation of a remarkable state of being.

I have touched upon grieving in this book and I wrote about it in *Little Miss Perfect*, but I believe the concept bears all the mention it can get. Grieving is a process through which we become able to stop feeling the pain of others (which, by the way, makes it impossible to say "No") and start feeling our own buried pain. It is through grief that we are able to realistically assess the past and thereby stop suffering from the intrusion, trauma, and abuse we were unable to feel. As the past comes into its true form we are able to connect buried feelings with memories; we stop having to hurt ourselves to avoid those feelings. It is through our knowing that we heal. Remember, the healing process of grief has its own timetable. We can only begin the work, and we cannot rush the process. It is what we hide from ourselves that can hurt us. Because we avoid the feelings that accompany loss and disappointment, we remain trapped in self-hatred and self-destruction. Compulsions and addictions prevent griefwork.

I have also talked about our beliefs and how they can keep us trapped in thought ruts. When we don't examine, update, and/or purge the file cabinets of our belief system, we run the risk of operating and making choices with out-of-date information. We react to situations with the mental attitude of a ten-year-old, forgetting completely that we are no longer that limited. Opportunities are missed by anyone who holds on to stale beliefs and refuses to investigate fresher territory. A healthy internal dialogue is curious, inquisitive, and full of learning experiences rather than being frightened and stuck.

When we walk around feeling afraid of everything and everybody, it is impossible to assess danger realistically and accurately. On the other hand, if we have so steeled ourselves from vulnerability that we are fearless, we don't believe that danger exists. Neither extreme is honest or involves living in the present moment. Both make it impossible to act in ways that are self-protective.

A healthy internal dialogue would not shout false fears at us. It can gently assure us and encourage us not to restrict our lives. A healthy internal dialogue can convince us that we have a healthy boundary and that nothing can hurt us as it did when we were children.

INTENTION AND ATTENTION

I have mentioned throughout this book that where we turn our attention has great significance for our well-being. The process of attending involves the selective narrowing of our focus of consciousness onto a particular event, person, thought, or sensation. Attending involves concentrating and remaining entirely in the present moment. As soon as we are yanked from the present by a memory (attention in the past) or anxiety (attention in the future) we lose the focus of our attention. Attending is like meditation; practice is the key.

Through the process of attending, our being becomes more receptive and therefore more vulnerable to the article of our attention. Some would say that we become more open. This receptivity voluntarily opens our emotional, spiritual, and intellectual boundaries and leaves us unguarded. This is why it is vitally important to our self-care that we consciously choose where we are going to place our attention.

Our day-to-day world is so filled with experiences, smells, sights, sounds, tastes, people, and places that it is difficult sometimes not to feel assaulted by everything that is out there. If our attention was sharply focused even most of the time, we would exhaust our energy and possibly our minds. This is one of the reasons people feel forced to blur their attention to some degree. It is when this blurring of attention becomes of greater importance than attending that we have crossed over into the arena of self-destructiveness. The act of blurring attention is analogous to numbing our senses and distorting the messages that come to us through our feelings and intuition. Numbing ourselves means that we are limiting our experiences. The motivation is fear.

Some of the ways in which people distort their attention include denial, substance abuse, and fantasy. By ignoring certain realities, people are able to forget that certain facts are true. They tell themselves the things they want to hear and further convince themselves that they are right. Unless the decision not to attend to certain realities is made consciously, as in the case of the woman who chose to stop reading the newspaper because the stories caused her such fear and anxiety, the element of choice gets lost. The woman who doesn't read the paper does not have her head completely in the sand; she keeps up with current events, but she has consciously chosen to lessen her fear and anxiety by refusing to submit herself to the stimulus of the newspaper. By contrast, someone who seeks to reduce the same fear and anxiety over conditions in the world by denying the realities that do exist is not making a conscious choice. He is refusing to believe the truth.

Substance abuse rarely begins as a conscious choice to numb attention, but it can emerge from a desire for relief from tension. Again we have the idea that there is a feeling or state of being that must be altered because it is "bad" or we don't like it. Rather than looking to find the causes and then trying to alter some of them, we do something to make it temporarily go away. Drugs and alcohol are a time-tested remedy. The surrounding culture reinforces the idea that the quick fix is always the best approach.

Fantasy is another avenue of escape for those seeking to distract their attention from what surrounds and threatens them. An acquaintance of mine was once described as a man "whose mind is so open that his brains have fallen out." Sadly, it was the truth. He was a well-educated, unemployed floater whose imagination generated very creative and eloquent fantasies. While he was a delight to experience in small doses, the truth of the matter was that he was not actually functioning at the level of a responsible adult. Without the generosity of caring friends he would have been on the street. The realities of work and responsibility were not within the scope of this man's perception. We all need to have enough access to our imagination to be able to use it for escape, but when we use it to escape to the point where we cannot return, we have literally gone too far.

So what makes the difference between conscious choice and unconscious action? I think the answer lies in the concept of intention. Intention can be described as determination to act as a result of attention that has been directed to a truth. Intention is the state of mind with which an act is done. It is the act of having one's mind, attention, or will concentrated on something, a specific end, a purpose. Intention is purposeful, specific, significant, and concentrated. Intention motivates every action, thought, and feeling we experience. This is why it is important to become aware of the intentions that influence our experiences.

If you think of intention in terms of cause and effect, you can begin to examine your experience and try to identify which intentions produce which effects. Once you have connected your honest intentions with the outcome, you can begin choosing intentions that produce effects you desire. Now, that may sound simple enough, but I'm afraid it isn't quite as easy as it sounds because of all the disinformation that we give ourselves, the ways in which we mask, disguise, and misinterpret our intentions in order to make them look like what we would like them to be. When we look at ourselves through the lens of the ideal image we have of ourselves, we are not seeing the true picture.

Let's go back to the example of the person who is doing everything she can to be pleasing to everyone around her. She works overtime trying to make people happy, anticipates and fulfills everyone's needs, and keeps conflict at a minimum. She may be wearing herself to a frazzle in her efforts, but what she experiences in return is that people continue being needy, she never does enough, no one is ever satisfied, and despite her valiant efforts to minimize the chances, conflicts arise.

So what is going on here? If we believe in the principle that what we consciously intend toward other people is what we experience as coming to us from them, then we can begin to look at this picture more honestly. It's the whole idea that what you put out is what comes back to you. Believing in this concept and operating out of it require tremendous self-responsibility and honesty.

The woman in our example thinks she is intending to please others. In fact, she experiences failure. Her flock is never-endingly needy. So, if we refocus our attention here and look at the situation from the point of view of what she is experiencing in return for her efforts, we see her intention as needing to fulfill her own needs by taking care of others. This shift reveals the actual intention that is being acted out in this situation. The real situation that exists within this woman is being projected outward through her actions toward others instead of being addressed internally as a personal issue. By refusing to acknowledge and take responsibility for her own needs this woman is not taking care of herself and is not being honest. She is attempting unsuccessfully to get her needs met by taking care of the needs of others. This is a boundary problem and a setup for defeat.

It is an extremely difficult and often uncomfortable process we must go through to become honest and responsible. That must be why we resort to the easier path of blaming and projecting our true feelings onto others. But once we have experienced the difference that authenticity can bring to our lives, we can begin to find the courage to do the work.

When you experience a particular emotion coming from another person—anger, hatred, envy, rejection, or fear—try shifting your attention to your own state of mind in regard to that person. The chances are good that your intention toward that person is exactly what you are experiencing in return, and the probability is high that you have been completely unaware of this.

Intention does not apply only to our interactions with people; it also applies to the way in which we live our lives, the choices that we make, and the process we go through in making those decisions. Until we can accurately focus our attention on the true intention of our choices, we will be acting dishonestly in the world. Conscious choice is the only way in which we can truly evolve, and as long as we choose self-destruction and dishonesty, we will remain splintered and damaged beings.

"SO WHAT DO I SAY?"

Have you ever wished you could come up with the exact "right" words or phrase to use that would make everything different? Have you ever called a friend, begging for suggestions, answers, and ideas for dealing with a particular situation or person? Have you ever waked up in the middle of the night with the insight that if you had just said _____, everything would have turned out better? I think we all, at one time or another, have had the experience of looking for ways to express ourselves and protect our boundaries. This collective searching is the reason I put the section of phrases in Chapter 3.

In the past few years, when I have shared these phrases with people, there has usually been a tremendous transfer of energy. People get excited; they feel full of power and possibility. Unconsciously people know that with phrases like these they can take better care of themselves. But as soon as the initial rush of energy passes, they get scared. Fear seeps in as the newly equipped person suddenly begins to imagine what will happen when he first uses one of these phrases. A harsh internal dialogue may pop up, shouting things like "You're such a bitch," "You can't say that to me," "You'll get fired for this," or even "How dare you?" And immediately we start to censor ourselves. We automatically begin taking care of other people's feelings and reactions at the expense of our own. This is the core of our self-destruction and the reason we must create healthier boundaries.

Imagine that we could shut down the internal dialogue that warns us of the doom that will surely follow our newfound self-assertion. Imagine that we could negotiate with this fearful voice and assure it that there are plenty of possibilities for outcomes and that more than half are positive. Imagine that we could stay so self-centered that we never even entertained the idea of how our words would be received. Imagine knowing that the importance lay in taking care of ourselves, honestly setting our boundaries, and letting others do the same for themselves. This is a fairly mind-boggling journey through the imagination for those of us with damaged boundaries. We are so well schooled in our self-denial that putting ourselves first is an unknown idea, something we have to deliberately set out to learn.

If someone walked past you and stole your wallet and ran off down the street, you would probably scream, maybe even chase after the robber and report the incident to the police. If someone struck and dented your automobile, you would react in anger, possibly yell at the offender, and definitely want to make sure there was insurance to cover the damages. Money and personal possessions seem to be the things that people are willing to risk confrontation over. But what if a friend calls and talks nonstop for forty-five minutes while you are trying to get ready for a trip out of town? As you listen, you are becoming anxious about packing, calling a taxi, and getting to the airport on time, but you say nothing to interrupt your friend. Or perhaps your supervisor at work has been harassing you lately. He stands closer to you than before, and there is sexual innuendo in everything that is said. You feel uncomfortable, but you say nothing.

It seems that we protect our possessions more easily than we protect ourselves. There is something very sad about this. Are not your feelings, your time, and your physical well-being deserving of the same defense you might provide for your wallet or your automobile? I think the answer is "Yes." First, we must learn how to say "No."

We must learn how to get around the inner guards who warn us of the dangers of speaking up for ourselves. Further, we must begin to generate new experiences for ourselves. Pick one of the phrases from chapter 3. Better yet, make up one of your own that suits a specific situation in your life and practice using it. If you need to devise a plan like the one I described that altered my automatic response to the real or imagined needs of others, then construct one for yourself. Figure out where you falter and design your plan to interrupt your pattern just slightly. Trying to make drastic changes in a big hurry is a strategy doomed to failure.

Personally I have found it necessary to have time and a little distance from any situation in order to differentiate my feelings from my reactions. Whenever we feel that our boundaries have been violated, we immediately begin to react. We may retreat, or we may arm ourselves in defense. If we can find that calm, safe space within our minds, that self-center, then we can collect our thoughts and feelings instead of continuing to react mindlessly. So maybe the first phrases you need to try out are ones that ask for time and space:

"I need a little time to think about that."
"I'll let you know what I think tomorrow."
"Let me sleep on it."
"I can't make a decision right now."
"I need to talk to some other people about this first."

Listen for the lines in movies and the passages in books that thrill you; you will know intuitively the phrases that ring true for you, that fill you with a sense of power and possibility. Practice this new language of self-assertion in front of the mirror. Practice them in simple situations that are not too threatening. If you need to, write your phrases down on pieces of paper so that you can cue yourself under stressful situations. As you begin to feel the increased energy and vitality that are available within healthy boundaries, your use of the new language will be reinforced.

I am including the following short piece of writing because I think it presents a way of creatively shifting our inner dialogue and acquiring new awareness and boundary skills. The piece is a personal myth that was written by a friend of mine during a time when she was exploring her ancestry in the process of understanding and rearranging some of her internal dialogue. I especially like myths because they exist in all cultures and throughout all time. I believe myths illustrate the truths of the human condition more directly and clearly than other forms of writing do. I think myths can even reveal truths that are unknown. My friend claims she gained a great deal of insight and power from writing her myth. You might want to try writing one of your own. It can be surprising to see what shows up.

WHERE "NO" COMES FROM

There was born, under the rising moon, a light-skinned child possessed of the knowledge of all things unspoken. She was the second-born daughter of Nanija, the goddess of the social world, and Sephera, one of the lesser gods of abandonment and neglect.

Nanija's own mother, Planera, in her youth had been a free-spirited nymph surrounded by restraint she could not abide. The gods had punished her by giving her a baby girl to care for. Planera, defiant as ever, turned her back on the child and strode boldly away, proclaiming, "No, no, no, I won't care for that baby. I won't take her home, I don't want her, and you cannot make me." Away she went.

So this precious child, Nanija, sent as an instrument of restraint by the gods, was brought to live in a motherless place where people were afraid to hold her. She could never escape the knowledge that she had failed in her earthly purpose, and she hardened herself against all weakness and tears. Her back grew straight, and her will solidified around her like a fortress.

In later years men thought Nanija was beautiful. She found men satisfyingly simple to control. She grew stronger in her goddess self as ruler of all things social.

A tall, silent man approached her and spoke of love. He was Sephera, the god of abandonment and neglect. Nanija recognized and loved him immediately, as though they had grown within one another's skin. Together they danced and ate and drank and drank and drank in the realm of the social world.

In one year Nanija bore a daughter whom she named for herself and set about shaping in her own image. But the child grew red and rugged and horrified the goddess, reminding her of failure. Despite her tireless efforts, Nanija could not mold this child into a presentable image of herself. So she turned her attention away. A second daughter came as a new challenge for Nanija. This fair child came brooding into the world on the rise of the moon. She was named Ariel.

Ariel began as a contest, an antagonism to her

mother. Nanija was frightened of this child, the power of her being, and the focus of her clear blue eyes. Ariel held a wisdom that Nanija couldn't have. Out of her fear Nanija devised her modifications. She would fill the child with fears to lessen her strength. Nanija wrapped her arms gently around the child and poured out her dread and worry into Ariel's infant ears. As the child grew, as if on parallel tracks, she heard her own voice and the mimicking voice of her mother arguing, always arguing inside.

When Ariel was still a child, Nanija banished Sephera and had a party. Inside the girl a great wound opened into which she shoved her rage at her mother's social distraction. She grew violent boils along her spine, screams of rage she would not share. She picked up the shield of invulnerability and held contempt against those who did not. She began to chant the tune of negativity that the women of her line sang. As she sang, she lost the sound of her own voice and drowned in the harsh voice of her inner Nanija.

Finally, as she grew into her young goddess self, her competitive and achieving nature stirred great conflict within her. A frightened voice breathed doubt and shame while her nature drove her to success and excellence. Her conflict drew her away from people, out of her mother's social arena, away from the noise and the distraction. The weight of her shield became heavier each day.

One night in a dream Planera visited her granddaughter. Ariel recognized her spirit at once. Planera urged the young goddess to follow her heart and learn how to enjoy her life. "I want to give you a treasure, something that you will have to learn how to use. The treasure is tiny, and you must not lose it. The treasure is 'No.' "

The next morning Ariel had no memory of her dream, but she felt a lightness and a hopefulness that were unaccustomed. She dressed and went for a walk along the mountain ridge. There she met a spider. In the past she would have killed the spider without a thought, but this morning she was curious and wanted to know this spider. She was not afraid.

The spider looked up into the clear blue light of Ariel's eyes and thanked her for her gentleness. "Most people kill us spiders without a second thought, but you have the gentleness of someone who cares."

Ariel sat down, reflecting on the change in herself. She held the spider up for examination, explaining, "I don't know what has come over me; this morning I am filled with a fascination for all life. There is no longer any fear in me, just a love that would not permit me to harm, much less kill, you. I have been given a gift that has changed my life."

The spider smiled at her and answered, "And it has changed mine as well."

CHAPTER 6

The Need for Action

I HAVE BEEN BUILDING AN ARGUMENT THAT STATES THAT A crisis in personal boundaries exists in our culture. A quick survey will convince you that we are under siege. Assault comes at us from the outside as noise, air and water pollution, psychological intrusion, and physical and sexual abuse. Internally we respond with anxiety, depression, obsession, addiction, and even suicide.

People are held hostage by their pain and fear, locked inside a prison where personal boundaries are blurred or completely obliterated. As the tension builds, they feel the need to take some action to alleviate the pressure. These actions generally involve some kind of physical act, such as aggression, substance abuse, and self-directed injury. Massive suffering is taking place because we have built and bought the myth of immediate gratification, the quick fix.

175

The statistics on addiction, violence, child abuse, and suicide all bear witness to the reality of this crisis. The current estimates show that sixty million Americans are sexual abuse survivors; seventy-five million of us have had our lives seriously affected by alcoholism; fifteen million families are overtly violent; and sixty percent of women and fifty percent of men have eating disorders.[1] Suicide is now considered a major public health problem in the United States. The only group in our society that has shown an increase in the mortality rate in the past twenty years has been those sixteen to twenty-four years old. Alcohol, drug-related accidents, homicides, and suicides are the major factors. Suicide is now the second greatest killer of people age ten to twenty-four. The first is automobile accidents, and it is unclear how many of those deaths may be suicides.[2]

People with addictions are methodically killing themselves every day without seeing it that way. Their unconscious minds are sending excuses to their conscious minds; self-destructiveness hides cleverly behind denial. Our society is in the fast lane to self-destruction.

In addition to the obvious clinical addictions, there are countless seemingly less harmful addictions, such as anger, excitement, orderliness, cleanliness, newness, and control, that hold people in their harmful grasp.

ADDICTION AND SELF-HARM

Habitual behaviors, whether they are substance-oriented or self-stimulating, all share the common ingredient of being driven by a person's desire to feel better. These habits reinforce themselves by reducing some discomfort originating from external events or internal conflict. Addictions have the distinction of being behaviors that are gratifying and punishing at the same time. All these behaviors give immediate but short-lived relief and end up being a problem. When the chosen behavior is engaged in, there is an initial state of euphoria, "the rush," followed by a slump. The slump feels bad again, and an urgent message is sent to repeat the original behavior. Over time, dependency develops and takes hold. Addiction is evident when one becomes progressively unable to control the beginning or the end of one's behavior, when choice has been forfeited. Compulsion, loss of control, and the continuation of a behavior despite harmful consequences are the criteria for addiction.

Addictions are self-destructive outgrowths of adaptive behaviors. Poor self-esteem and a lack of competence certainly contribute to dependence on any mood-altering activity. Childhood experiences can pattern how an adult will react under pressure. Genetic predispositions can determine the probability of addictive behavior.

Biological, psychological, and complex social forces drive us to alter our feelings, to actually change the way messages are sent and received by our brains. When the force of facts is too direct and brutal to be ignored, our awareness can distort the meaning. Through denial and self-deception any individual can deaden his pain by warping his awareness. There is a delicate balance between awareness and anxiety. Endorphins are the neurotransmitters, or communication system, between cells in the brain. They work to relieve pain that is triggered by physiological causes, apprehension (threat of pain), or psychological stress. Endorphins block our attention in such a way that pain does not register with full force. People who are risk takers or who are addicted to excitement and crisis use endorphins to keep their pain-awareness scale out of balance. While they keep the endorphin level high, they feel no pain. This is quite a lot to do in order to feel better.

Many people actually disfigure themselves in the process of trying to escape feelings of intolerable tension, frightening emptiness, or inexpressible anger. They engage in dangerous and harmful behaviors as a form of self-stimulation, and in the process they cause themselves harm. People who engage in self-mutilation are activating their endorphins with each brutal act. When individuals cause themselves physical disfigurement and pain, we are seeing human behavior at its worst, its most extreme.

It is estimated that twenty to twenty-five percent of all adults are active nail biters, which includes those who pick at the cuticles and at patches of uneven skin around the nails.[3] This behavior serves the dual purpose of being simultaneously disturbing and perversely satisfying. Almost all nail biters would agree that they have developed an array of defensive techniques for hiding the biting and the aftereffects of their work. It is a behavior seemingly without rationalization and one that carries tremendous shame. People manage to rationalize various addictions and compulsions: "I only drink in the evening," "It keeps the house clean, doesn't it?" or "It's not hurting anyone else, and I feel fine." The excuses for the temptations of the culture include physical

gratification—"I like it"—and overall manageabil-
ity—"I can handle it." But for those who chew their
nails, the habit seems to have no point, no worthwhile
purpose.

Deliberate self-mutilation is difficult to understand,
since it runs counter to the normal human preference for
avoiding pain and seeking pleasure. Statistics indicate
that the incidence of self-mutilative behaviors has increased markedly since the 1960s, and it is still thought
to be highly underreported. The current estimates are
between 14 and 600 cases per 100,000 people per year.
These behaviors include those mentioned above and the
more severe cases of wrist cuts, tattoos, cigarette burns,
chronic hair pulling, scalp irritation, excessive body
piercing, chewing the inside of the mouth or another
body part, excessive skin picking, putting one's eye out,
mutilating genitals, and amputating body parts. It is
shocking the lengths to which we will go to escape our
feelings and dull our awareness.[4] Cigarette smoking
could certainly be added to the list of acts of deliberate
self-harm. The package itself contains severe health
warnings that people ignore whenever they pick up the
pack and light up.

So how can we stop harming ourselves? How can we
rid ourselves of our addictions and compulsions? How
can we stand by our feelings and survive? I think the
answer lies with our attention and how we use it. We
cannot hope to say "No" to thoughts and behavior of
which we are unaware or that we refuse to admit are
harmful.

DENIAL

I have mentioned denial, and much has been written about it in the past few years, but it is such a pernicious demon that I believe it must be kept constantly before one's eyes. The second we forget its power, the more determined and detrimental becomes its work.

Denial serves the same basic function as the neurotransmission of endorphins: it provides temporary relief from pain. Denial is the psychological way in which we alter our attention, the way we tune out. Both the endorphin pain-suppression system and the mechanism of denial have great value in emergencies: they protect us from too much awareness and too much pain. However, in the long run neither is the right choice for an honest recovery. The ways in which we interpret the experiences and events of our lives determine whether they are stressful. Threat is not inherent in every situation, yet the perception of threat is produced by our appraisal. Our experience is shaped by the back-and-forth shift between pain and attention. When we use our attention to skew our awareness and deny a threat, we can protect ourselves from ensuing feelings of pain and anxiety. Our constant drive to avoid pain keeps us from ever learning what is true about ourselves.

One way in which we distort our attention is by developing mind-sets. A mind-set is a way to avoid being present and aware of a particular experience. By deciding beforehand how we are going to feel or react, we do not have to experience the event in the moment. We need only follow our prescribed reaction, our mind-set. Through this mechanism we avoid having to be present and authentic. Our response is preplanned, perhaps even rehearsed. We pass through our experiences untouched, numb.

Many of us still operate from under the guise of the perfect veneer. The truth is too ugly and painful to acknowledge; it doesn't look like the image of ourselves we can accept, so we project a false image. We ignore and deny what doesn't fit with our false self-image. Self-deceptions and psychological defenses work to preserve and protect our denial. As long as these mechanisms operate below the level of conscious awareness, they set the limits for our thoughts, feelings, perceptions, and actions.

Many of the limits we accept, the messages we give ourselves, such as "I could never do that" and "Only really smart guys can do that," are not necessarily the truth. We may have unconsciously adopted the labels others put on us as children—"She is not working up to her potential"—and limited our competency in accordance with them. Possibly if those labels were brought to the level of consciousness where awareness could scrutinize them, we would make other choices. It is through deliberate attention that we can regain our alternatives and choices.

MAKING CHOICES IN THE PRESENT

Attention is sort of a slippery concept to hold on to. We are admonished in school to "Pay attention," and all through life we are given messages: "Beware" (be aware), "Keep your eyes open," and "Stay sharp." These messages sound more like warnings than like invitations to the most rewarding and exciting activity in life—being aware.

Attention can be described as the constant gathering of information that is required for existence. It is the information we receive through our senses, and it is the information that comes to us from the more mysterious realms of our intuition and imagination. Wherever our attention is focused is where we are headed. If we choose to attend to the negative aspects of life, the pain and weakness, the disappointment and the longing, we will operate out of a framework that reflects our beliefs. Negativity breeds its own energy field; we can choose to surround ourselves with it, and we can choose not to. Our experiences are shaped by the choices we make.

If we allow ourselves to passively absorb information without scrutinizing it, we will wind up using that information in an unconscious manner in the future. This is the nature of fear, hatred, and discrimination. However, if we are thoughtful about what information we allow into our minds, we can be thoughtful about the way in which we use that information. This is the essence of caring and compassion.

Habits are activities or beliefs that take place below our awareness. Their repetition is like a low drumbeat that we do not notice in the music. The beat is constantly there, but we are unaware of it. To change a belief or habit, one's attention must be turned from the melody to the bass beat, and the volume must be turned up. Only when reality is brought to the level of conscious activity can we begin to exert our powers of choice and modification.

Our society rewards singularity of focus. We are

trained and reinforced in the pursuit of outcomes. Focused people are labeled "industrious, purposeful, dedicated, hardworking, and successful," while those of us who see more choices are labeled "scattered, flighty airheads" or, worst of all, "artistic." In this relentless dedication to outcomes, the value of process, how we get to outcomes, is lost. The rich diversity of processes is not honored; instead, we are encouraged to pick a single pursuit and stick to it until we have accomplished it. The processes of exploration and discovery are forfeited for the all-powerful outcome. Not only are the pleasures of curiosity and diversity lost in this pursuit, the boundaries of possibility become narrow and limited. Outcome orientation does not encourage alternative ways of thinking. It is just like overly protective parents who cannot tolerate the mistakes along the path of learning that their children make. The culture reinforces the message that the end result is what counts, not what is learned along the way.

How we define an activity determines the energy we have available to bring to it. If we categorize something as a chore, we will feel tired, obligated, disinterested, or imposed on. Conversely, if we envision an activity as an adventure, we will have enthusiasm, resourcefulness, and energy to spare. It is important to examine our categories, to see how we define certain things to ourselves. Are these categories of our own design? We do have control over the way we look at things as long as we remember to hold on to it. It is with this ability to look at old, familiar problems in new, fresh ways that we find liberation from our obsessions, compulsions, and addictions.

In addition to changes in attitude, we have the power to change aspects of ourselves that are harmful or unsatisfactory. Whenever we forget this power and hand it over to others, when we label others as "experts" in our lives, we have made the mistake once again of looking on the outside for the quick fix. In so doing, we deny the knowledge that comes from our intuition.

Memory is attention in the past, and it is subject to distortion just as attention is. If your attention is focused on memory, you are essentially living in the past, dwelling on what happened then. Your attention is not readily available for you to use in the present. Similarly, anxiety is attention in the future; it is the feeling evoked by the threat of uncertainty. Anxiety gets caught up with "What if?" and "If only." Without careful attention and some discipline, virtually all our thoughts are based either in the past or in the future. All our fears and desires are there, too. Consequently, whenever we are focused on our desires or fears, we are incapable of living in the present moment. Memory and anticipation rob us of the richness and experience of the present moment. Bringing attention back into the present ultimately increases our levels of awareness and self-knowledge. Even if everything we discover is not to our liking, living in the present is the only way we can hope to become aware of our personal boundaries, protect them, and begin to shed our self-destructive tendencies. When we truly see ourselves clearly in the bright light that shines once denial has been lifted, we can begin to make responsible choices and, through those choices, participate in our evolution.

I once heard author and lecturer Stephen Levine refer

to human beingness as "the suffering for which we took birth to heal."[5] By healing I don't believe he meant finding a cure or medicating the pain that comes in life. He was talking about the spiritual process of gaining balance with our true nature, finding that peaceful harmony with which our personality and our soul can relax. It is only when these two parts of our being are not at war that basic human kindness toward ourselves and others can emerge. Levine spoke of how our self-image causes us to suffer. We lock our true selves out of our hearts, out in the cold somewhere, and project onto the world a lawyer or a teacher, a mother or a father, some identity, an "I am"–ness that separates us from our true selves and from a power greater than ourselves. Our personality is firmly attached to our identity, how we describe and present ourselves to the outside world. It is this strong ego attachment that causes our suffering.

Levine explained that the experience of am-ness is basically the same for everyone regardless of his apparent station in life. This is because am-ness is our shield, our protection, our grief. Letting go of our suffering is the hardest work we are ever asked to do. We are all attached to and deeply invested in our self-images. The possibility of losing those self-images feels too devastating for most of us, so we work overtime to protect them and to shield ourselves. In reality the fear of the unknown is just that, fearful. Ultimately, it is through our willingness to embrace fear that we begin to grow and make room for new awareness. Looking beyond our fear facilitates our transcendence of identity; it allows us to communicate with our innermost part, the soul, our higher self, God, whatever you want to call it.

Fear is what keeps us trapped in our addictions. Truthfully facing our self-images and seeing through them to our authentic selves is the healing work for our spiritual boundaries. Compassion and awareness are the pathways to healing our suffering. They are the steps required for shedding our attachment to our am-ness and ego, ultimately leading us to reclaim our unique beingness, or spirituality.

INTUITION AND ASSUMPTION

Intuition is our communication system with the nonphysical world. It is not necessarily conscious, and it may reveal itself through dreams, insights, or just bright moments of knowingness. Intuition extends beyond the information that comes to us through our senses; it is not always rational and is hard to explain to those who demand rationality. As such, intuition is not highly regarded in our society. "Women's intuition" is both ridiculed and jealously regarded by the culture.

Imagination is a vital ingredient in human beings' adaptation on this planet. Without imagination, inventions would never have been made and the species probably would not have survived. Imagination is what allows us to explore our relationship to the world and whatever lies beyond. Imagination, when it is working in our behalf, helps us feel safe and protected in a benevolent universe. When imagination is not working in our behalf, we are convinced of all dangers and run in a panic from our vulnerability. Intuition is imagination that is used in a very focused and controlled way. It all goes back to attention, how and where it is placed.

It is through intuition that the earthbound personality can begin to make connections with powers greater than itself, with guides and teachers, angels, and our higher selves.

Let me stop here for a moment to discuss something, this power greater than the self, to which I have been alluding. Sooner or later people suffering from various addictions will undoubtedly come into contact with the 12-step program that originated with Alcoholics Anonymous. These steps are the spiritual foundation for the work of recovering from addiction. If these principles are incorporated in an addict's life and beliefs, he becomes able to cease relying on a substance, a behavior, or a fantasy for comfort. Many people who are not alcoholics or drug addicts have found these steps helpful for developing and living happy and effective lives. It is my personal bias that everyone could benefit from exploring the meaning of these spiritual principles and examining how they could apply to their lives.

The second step of AA reads, "Came to believe that a power greater than ourselves could restore us to sanity." For some, this higher power, or power greater than ourselves, is known as God, but for many the concept of God has been damaged, ignored, or discarded altogether. *God* is a term burdened by religious dogma, especially for people who were shown a harsh, punishing, and all-knowing God. Then there are people who believed in a kind and benevolent God but whose lives have been so difficult that their beliefs have been shattered. For some the notion of God has changed from a patriarchal overlord to a gentler feminine, life-promoting goddess. Or perhaps the idea of God has been replaced by a void, a belief in nothing.

Regardless of your religious experiences, the 12-step spiritual program maintains that until you become aware of and accept the presence of a power greater than yourself, you will be held hostage to the power of addiction, self-deception, and self-destruction. It is the acceptance of a power greater than ourselves that allows us to begin releasing our ironclad grip on the notion that we are alone in the world and have to do everything on our own. Accepting a power greater than ourselves expands our options and alternatives. It is also lightens our burden of responsibility and guilt.

Intuition is one avenue of communication between the self and a power greater that the self. Intuition is a power of attention capable of receiving direct knowledge or cognition without evident rational thought or interference. In reality there is quite a bit of interference put up by the culture, which keeps us distracted from inner knowing and casts doubt on any knowledge that goes beyond rational thought. Nonetheless, intuition survives.

I remember one very vivid piece of absolutely irrefutable evidence that proved to me that help is available if we can ask for it, wait, and be willing to accept what comes. I was at a point of great confusion and despair. I felt that I had run out of options for patience in a situation that was building in its destructiveness. I didn't know what to do. Feeling utterly exhausted, I put my head down on my desk and said out loud, "I don't know what to do. Please send me some help." Literally within a minute a car drove into the driveway. My first reaction was "Oh, no, I don't want to see anyone right now," but I went downstairs and met a friend at the back door. He didn't give any particular reason for having stopped by. In fact, both of us acted uncomfortable, sort of like neither one of us knew why we were there. I was remembering my request for help when I asked him, "What are you doing here?" He answered, "I'm not quite sure. I just felt like coming over to see how you were doing." I felt in that moment that I was being cared for, directly by my friend but even more directly by a power greater than myself to whom I had turned for assistance. I hugged my friend, and we sat on the front porch and talked for hours. It was exactly what I needed.

There are, if we can recognize them, countless examples throughout our lives in which unexpected turns were taken, losses were suffered that turned out for the best, or mistakes added up to the perfect solution. It is through our ability to not fight but rather to accept these twists of fate that we learn to accept the guidance and protection of a power greater than ourselves. If we cannot be flexible and accepting, if we are forced to rigidly control the events and people in our lives in accordance with our expectations, our passage through life will be a bumpy one.

If one accepts the notion of guidance from a greater source, then the flow of that guidance will be smooth. But if one blocks awareness of a power greater than the self through willfulness, denial, or addiction, then guidance must come through physical events. If this is the case, if guidance is being blocked, the lessons that lead to awareness may take the form of a crisis. Crisis necessitates that choices be made; it stretches human potential to its extreme. The crisis-oriented teaching process is slow, and some people never get the message that help is available if one will only become willing to accept it. A person without guidance from intuition and the power greater than the self has no choice but to wind up in crisis. It is these crises that provide opportunities to discard patterns of thought and behavior that are no longer necessary or useful. Failure to recognize and act on these opportunities will lead one right back into the same cycle. Thus the addict who gets sober and falls off the wagon, the overeater who loses weight only to gain it back, the relationship addict who keeps having the same relationship with different people. Ignoring our opportunities to learn makes it impossible to grow and evolve and condemns us to a cycle of repetition.

So what keeps us from being able to access our intuition and learn from the opportunities we are given? I think the answer is fear. We are afraid of facing and admitting our powerlessness and vulnerability. We are afraid of facing our pain. It is difficult to take full responsibility for the self-destructive choices we may have made, but the harm in holding on is worse than the pain of letting go.

Fear of pain and fear of letting go prevent us from learning from our past experiences and keep us trapped into repeating them. Fear keeps us trapped in our addictions. Author Anne Wilson Schaef states it this way: "When we do not know our own boundaries, when we perceive the world as either for us or against us, when we never have enough of anything, we cannot help but be fearful."[6] Until we can face the fear, learn our lessons, and move on, we will be trapped in a cycle of repetition. Until we learn from our opportunities, we are doomed to visit them over and over again. Furthermore, without an awareness of our fears we remain incapable of experiencing compassion, the truthful experience of authenticity that enables us to stop hating and punishing ourselves.

One of the ways in which we interfere with the awareness that can come from intuition is making assumptions. To assume is to literally take possession of the supposition of truth, or to take the truth for granted. To my mind, both of these actions constitute boundary invasions. In the first instance—"taking possession"— the truth is being invaded and captured. In the second the truth is being taken for granted rather than honored.

Have you ever had the experience of a close friend making an assumption on your behalf that was totally out of line with what you would have chosen for yourself if you had been given the choice? How did you feel in that instance? My experiences have left me with the memory that such intrusions on my ability to state my own preferences or needs are highly irritating and generally incorrect. It is often said, "To assume makes an *ass* of *u* and *me*." I think that is the truth.

Just as denial is attention based on avoidance, assuming is attention based on invasion. Making assumptions is a boundary violation and is disrespectful of another person's autonomy. Assuming we know what is best for other people, what they would like or how they feel, involves putting ourselves in a position of being all-knowing, superior, or one up. We are not allowing the other person to speak or think for himself, to state his own preferences and feelings. We are treating these people like children. If they aren't children, this is not a loving attitude to take. It is condescending, arrogant, intrusive, and most certainly unloving.

Once more we have to look at the idea of intention. When we assume on someone else's behalf, we are rarely aware of our underlying intention to take control of that person or assure that our needs are met without opposition. But in actuality assuming is a way of maintaining control, of projecting our own will onto another person and pretending we thought it was his. Assumptions support our addictions and self-destructive behaviors. They are a way of distorting reality and distracting our awareness from what is actually true. Assumptions are a way of lying to ourselves and to others.

Sometimes we disguise our intentions under the well-meaning cloak of not wanting to hurt other people's feelings. But when we are assuming, we are literally stealing their feelings, and our rationale is just a means for protecting our need to control.

Making assumptions is another way of avoiding the present moment and distorts straightforward communication. Assuming prevents intimacy. When we focus outwardly onto others, it is impossible to remain focused on ourselves, our needs, our reality, and our pain. When we cannot be honest with ourselves, we cannot hope to connect with other people.

Intuition is one way of having greater access to the awareness that comes from within and from a power greater than ourselves. Assumption is a way of staying out of touch with a power greater than ourselves and imagining that we are a power greater than others. Assumption is born out of the fear of loss and the fear of not getting what we want. Intuition is reverent; assumption is restricting.

When we imagine how others are going to respond to our self-assertions without giving them a chance to do so, we are intruding on their boundaries and failing to protect our own.

EXERCISE

Imagine three people with whom you have trouble stating your true feelings and desires. Write their names down on a piece of paper. Next, write down each of the phrases from Chapter 3, plus any that you have added, on another piece of paper. On a third piece of paper write down what you fear would be the responses of each of the three people to any and all of the self-assertion statements. Here is an example:

"I don't want to talk about this right now."
Father would say, "Now, listen here, you can't talk to
    me like that."
"I don't care what you want to or don't want; you sit
    down and listen to me."
"Who died and made you God?"
Steve would say (sarcastically), "So, when would be
    a good time, Your Highness?"
"Well, excuuuuuse me!"
"Oh, right, I forgot to raise my hand."
Mother would say, "You can't talk to me like that."
"What makes you so special?"

Continue until you have exhausted all the responses you can think of that might interfere with your new attempts at self-assertion. When you have finished, take the third piece of paper, the one with their responses, and destroy it. I suggest burning it, but if burning is not safe or possible, then tear the paper into tiny pieces and get rid of them.

You need to be rid of these presumed responses because they are what keep you from standing up for yourself and defending your boundaries. Even if the people wouldn't actually say the things you have written, your fear that they will makes the responses just as real as if you had actually heard them.

If you have more than three people with whom you have trouble establishing and maintaining healthy boundaries, and most of us do, then repeat the exercise, three at a time, until you have covered the important people in your life. Remember, learning new skills is a matter of practice.

BARRIER OR BOUNDARY

I recently overheard a couple talking and was struck once again by the complexity of this thing called setting boundaries. The following is my analysis of the situation that occurred. There are, of course, other conclusions that could be drawn, but this is how I saw it.

This man and woman met in a teacher-student format and became friends and later lovers. The man, who had been the teacher, is also twenty or more years older than the woman. In terms of their peerness this couple has the constant backdrop of status differential and age difference.

The conversation I observed took place one morning as the woman was reading and the man was having coffee. He is watching her, then asks, "What are you learning from what you are reading?"

Her back stiffens, and she looks up slowly from the pages of the book. "What do you mean?" she asks with an irritated look on her face.

"What are you getting out of the book?" He repeats his original question.

At this point I am empathizing with the woman, who I suspect is feeling both intruded on and quizzed by her former teacher.

She mumbles something vague in a soft voice, then looks directly at him and says, "I'd really rather just keep reading and not talk about it right now."

Internally I am cheering. Here is a woman who can do exactly what I am talking about in this book: she can clearly and kindly set her boundaries. I am impressed.

He, however, perhaps feeling rebuked, keeps pushing. He obviously wants to make some connection. He responds, "Why are you shutting me out? Why are you putting this barrier between us?"

She, looking frustrated and on the verge of defeat, answers, "I don't want to fight about this. I just want some peace and quiet."

At this point I am sure that the interaction I am observing has more to do with something I am not seeing than with something I am. The emotions are running higher than the current situation would suggest. The

man is angry and goes outside to smoke a cigarette. The
woman resumes reading her book.

It seemed to me that he labeled her boundary as a
barrier and thereby turned it into something bad. This is
a difficult concept to deal with in setting boundaries for
oneself. The probability that someone else will not like
being put off, left out, or denied in any way is very
high. It is a rare individual who has enough of a sense
of self to graciously accept "No" as an answer. This is
because "No" feels like a rejection. It goes back to the
idea that "No" had come to mean "I don't like you" or
"That's a stupid idea."

If this scene had been played out with another
woman who had less defined boundaries, she might
have stopped what she was doing and attempted to
comfort the man, tried to effect a reconciliation. The
woman in question, however, was certain that she had
not been abusive in her remarks and felt she had no
need to soothe his feelings or worry about his reaction.
He had taken her clear request to be left alone personally, and she was not going to take responsibility for his
behavior. He had internalized her message as a personal
affront and reacted accordingly. He had been unable to
respect her boundary; instead, he framed it as a rejection of him. This is a very common problem when people do not communicate in a healthy manner.

The truth of the matter is that he wanted to connect
with this woman in some way. But rather than asking
her for some time and attention, he asked her a question, put her on the spot. Instead of honestly stating his
needs, he intruded on her quiet reading. This is why she
put him off. Then, feeling hurt and rejected, he at-

tacked. He labeled her behavior as setting a barrier between them, then retreated to further avoid his true feelings by smoking a cigarette.

As long as we are unable to get in touch with our true feelings, state them in an honest and straightforward manner, realize and cope with the fact that we sometimes will be disappointed and sometimes will get things different from what we expect, and respect our own boundaries and those of other people, we will be doomed to hiding and protecting ourselves with addictions. One of the characteristics of an addict is that he has almost no ability to differentiate between different feelings. Joy, anger, happiness, terror, anxiety, and boredom are all mixed up in a toxic mass of something to be shut off, pushed down, and blocked off. Unless we can learn to communicate honestly with ourselves and other people, we will be unable to connect with anything but our self-destructiveness. And until we learn to differentiate between responsibility and blame, we will not be able to establish healthy boundaries.

RESPONSIBILITY AND BLAME

People with unhealthy boundaries have tremendous confusion in regard to the issues of responsibility and blame. The two seem to be inextricably intertwined, and avoidance of blame precludes taking responsibility for actions or feelings. We see this dynamic in action in the earlier scenario in which Jamie asks Alan not to interrupt her when she is on the phone. Alan's defensive reaction is an indication that rather than taking responsibility for his behavior and attempting to modify it on the basis of a reasonable request from Jamie, he is feeling blamed for being a bad person and is therefore compelled to defend himself. Alan doesn't have a secure enough sense of himself to be able to hear that Jamie is merely making a request that he can choose to honor or not.

When a child experiences trauma, he develops defense mechanisms that minimize the chances of experiencing that trauma again. Various experiences and feelings produce different defense mechanisms. Feelings of shame are the primary source for the defense mechanism of blaming others. This defensive maneuver works to deflect responsibility onto other people because the blamer feels overburdened by shame. An example would be a young man who is caught shoplifting. When asked why he was stealing, his response is "I didn't do anything wrong; that stupid security guard just has it in for me. He is lying."

Shame is a belief system that is learned in childhood. Many things can fill a child with shame. Some common sources are relentless criticism, sexual abuse, and abandonment. As shame manifests itself in adulthood, it can be quite difficult, tainting interpersonal relations and making intimacy practically impossible. Adult experiences have to pass through the heavy fog of childhood shame and often emerge distorted. People who are consumed by the notion of their unworthiness have very weak personal boundaries. They feel threatened by other people and must always be on the defensive. They hear the feelings and requests of other people as indictments and criticism of themselves.

Shame develops from feeling rejected, neglected, or

abandoned in childhood. Therefore, it is not surprising that people with lots of shame do not respond well to hearing "No." Similarly, people with lots of shame have difficulty saying "No" to others because their low self-esteem tells them that they are not worthy, they do not deserve to be able to set limits, and saying "No" would only hurt somebody's feelings.

Responsibility and blame are not the same thing. To think so is to revert to the competitive mind-set that states that someone has to be wrong in order for me to be right. Responsibility means the ability to respond, to make an answer, to say something in return. There is no indication in this definition that anything wrong has taken place. Blame, on the other hand, means to find fault with. It also means to hold responsible for, but only after the fault has been found. Responsibility for a fault does not presume blame, merely accountability.

Is it any wonder that we are confused about the difference between responsibility and blame when we heard things like "Who is responsible for the crayon marks on the wall?" The question really meant who was to blame because in this instance there was fault and someone would probably wind up being punished. Who would ever want to take responsibility for anything if all it meant was that one was going to be blamed and punished?

The problem with not taking responsibility for our actions and feelings is that someone has to be responsible. It is not possible for there to be a responsibility void. Therefore, if we are not taking responsibility for ourselves, we must be assigning that responsibility to someone or something else. Then, depending on how

we are feeling and what we are experiencing, we are
adoring, ignoring, or blaming the people and things
around us.

On the other side of the coin are those people who
take too much responsibility. When responsibility is all
twisted up with blame, they feel guilty for things that
are beyond their control. I caught myself in one of these
whirlpools recently. Last summer I planted some bushes
in the front of the house. It was a very dry summer and
I wanted the new plants to establish healthy root systems, so I watered the plants very carefully all summer
and fall. In the late fall a storm came through, blowing
salt ashore, and burned the leaves on some of the
bushes. My immediate response was that I had to be
doing something wrong, conveniently forgetting all
about the storm and its impact on the plants. It took
some mental health housecleaning before I managed to
convince myself that the bushes were still alive and that
when the weather warmed up, new leaves would grow
in. I was all right for a few weeks until someone com-
mented that the bushes in the front looked pretty
ragged. Rather than being able to hear this comment as
a simple statement of the truth (they did look ragged),
I heard that I was doing a bad job taking care of the
plants and as a result they were dying. I responded to
the comment as though I had been attacked. In fact, I
had been—only the attack had been self-inflicted. My
sense of overresponsibility and my false belief that I am
to blame for things beyond my control ganged up on me
and won.

People who blame often do not take responsibility for
their actions and feelings, but those who take blame

often apologize for things that have nothing to do with them. The blamed are so filled with shame that every bad thing that happens must surely be their fault. Another common characteristic is that these people quickly back off from their stated opinions. They have no confidence in their feelings or beliefs and readily accept someone else's premise without even questioning it. This is certainly indicative of poor boundaries. People who cannot take responsibility for their own decisions easily capitulate to the will of others. This acquiescent behavior can put one in great danger of victimization.

By contrast, people who take on too much responsibility violate other people's boundaries by making assumptions for and about them. These people have a strong need to always be right, and as a result they cannot always listen to what other people are telling them. These people also tend to see the world through dualistic lenses: all good or all bad, wrong or right, black or white. Their need to be right tends to make them blame other people whenever they feel the slightest threat; they are constantly on the defensive. They take everything personally because they believe they are responsible for all of it. They have poor boundaries and a pervasive sense of impending doom.

It is crucial to untangle responsibility from blame and begin to see them as distinct concepts. Establishing healthy boundaries and breaking the cycle of addiction will require taking responsibility for our actions, but until we remove the weight of blame, we cannot hope to coax ourselves to do so.

EXERCISE

In the process of trying to shed some of my overly responsible beliefs, I once made up a job description that clearly outlined my responsibilities, those things for which I could be held accountable. After I finished this list of specific responsibilities, I made another list of those times when I feel blamed. I spent a lot of time on this second list. When it was done, I began a third list, and this was perhaps the most informative. The third list was for all the things that are *not* my responsibility. It is the second list that I must frequently refer back to when I am feeling the familiar tug of guilt that signals that I feel overly responsible for something beyond my control. You may want to try making up some lists like this for yourself. Here are some examples:

I am responsible for
My emotional, physical, and spiritual well-being
Conducting myself honestly in all my affairs
Establishing and maintaining my boundaries
My feelings

> *I feel blamed when*
> I disappoint others
> Other people are not having a good time
> Anyone is angry

>> *I am not responsible for*
>> The weather
>> Disappointment
>> Other people's reactions or feelings
>> Everyone having a good time

INTIMACY AND AUTONOMY

A delicate balance is established when people draw together for the purposes of friendship or love. This balance involves issues related to autonomy and intimacy. In this balancing act, either directly or indirectly, much is communicated about personal boundaries.

People whose boundaries have been damaged by physical, sexual, and emotional abuse may have a very strong need for autonomy. In the past they were subjected to the intrusions and desires of those who abused them. They felt powerless to alter their situations. Later, as adults, many found that the only way to feel safe is to have complete control over as many aspects of their lives as possible. The ultimate right of self-government that autonomy provides makes individuals feel less threatened by intrusion from the outside. Thoughts of intimacy or vulnerability raise a frightening specter of self-annihilation. These are the people it is hard to get to know. They may be good at setting limits and boundaries, but they set them far out in the distance. Or possibly they are not good with boundaries, so they isolate themselves to the point where they are never faced with the requests and demands of others.

However, other people who have suffered the same abuses may have forfeited so much of their autonomy that the thought of being alone is terrifying. These people are attracted to lovers and friends who continue the abuse, who abandon and neglect them or scream at and beat them. The pull of dependency is stronger than any independent urge toward self-protection. These are the battered women who hate the abuse but cannot leave

because "I love him." These are the men who go from
woman to woman because they are so unhappy with
themselves. Self-annihilation is what is unconsciously
sought in these intimate relationships. True sharing cannot actually take place in either of these cases because
two complete people are never participating.

For those people who can and do establish intimacy
there often comes a certain point when we worry that
we'll be swallowed up by the partner.

One morning a wife wakes up and realizes she is
tired of wearing the clothes her husband likes, especially since they are not the clothes she likes. She sadly realizes that she has sacrificed part of herself in order to
please; she has not honored her boundary. One friend
complains to another, "We always do what you want to
do. Why can't we ever do what I want?" Or a husband
looks around the table at his family and feels trapped:
his life is over, and it wasn't any fun. It is at these
points that friends and lovers are challenged. The question becomes one of how to be a distinct and separate
individual (autonomous) and still remain emotionally
attached to the other person (intimate). Unfortunately,
these points often are reached when couples decide to
split up. The wife decides she has sacrificed too much
to ever get it back, so she ends the marriage, cleans the
slate, and starts all over with her self-definition. The
friend whose needs never get met decides she isn't really getting anything out of this friendship and moves
on to another one. The husband who feels life is at an
end turns to a younger woman to help him feel revital-
ized. These are the stories we hear every day, and they

are related to this delicate balancing of intimacy and autonomy.

When two people who have enough self-esteem not to fear self-annihilation come together as friends or lovers and are able to maintain their individual distinctiveness within the partnership, they are then confronted with the challenge of facing their internal conflicts. These are healthy people who can focus on another person while remaining connected to themselves. They are not like the people who get "swept away" or "lose themselves" in the company of another. The romantic fantasy of everything being perfect when Mr. or Ms. Right comes along is not adhered to by these honest partners. They do not look for all their needs to be fulfilled by someone else, and they do not deny and ignore any of their feelings. At the same time they are aware of, without intruding on or being overly responsible for, the feelings of the other.

Intimacy and autonomy are enhanced when friends and lovers can honestly share any and all of their feelings without fear of being rejected, ignored, converted, or healed. It is completely satisfying to feel that one has simply been heard, more satisfying than being given suggestions is. Making suggestions or trying to "fix" other people's problems is an invasion of autonomy and a violation of intimacy. In short, it is a boundary trespass.

When individuals can recognize and accept their feelings as originating within themselves and then share them with a partner, they are honoring the self and are trusting enough to reveal it to another. In relationships where this honest sharing can be received without the

perception of threat, manipulation, or guilt, the boundaries surrounding autonomy and intimacy are held sacred
and the boundaries between people are distinct.

The integration of autonomy and intimacy within an
individual is an important step toward a person's ability
to be vulnerable with others. When we are unconsciously afraid of being consumed or rejected, we cannot feel safe enough to reach out and make contact.
When we cannot accept "No" as a possible answer, we
don't allow other people to be themselves. In the process of regaining the ability to be honest and vulnerable, we begin making meaningful connections with
people. Whether people are friends, lovers, coworkers,
or parents, their personal boundaries will be respected.
This is a desirable and rewarding outcome for all the
work and terror involved with personal discovery, self-
negotiation, and self-acceptance. Furthermore, integration and wholeness within a person can translate into
relationship. With healthier personal boundaries people
are safer and hurt themselves and others less often; as
people they begin to draw together, and the world begins to heal as well.

CHAPTER 7

Letting Go Doesn't Mean Having Nothing to Hold On To

$\mathcal{W}$HENEVER I AM STANDING ON THE BRINK OF A MAJOR change in my life, as when I am standing before the abyss of possibility and growth, I feel terror. Making changes, letting go of old habits of thought and behavior, is a frightening and chaotic enterprise. That is why people work so hard to distract themselves from the awareness that changes need to be made. It is why most people remain addicted to substances, activities, and other people rather than chosing to live their lives fully. Ultimately it is fear that separates us from other people, keeps us hiding behind walls of protection, and erects barriers to our experience of life. Fear produces all of our supposedly self-protective disguises, and it must be released in order to heal ourselves, our communities, and the world. It is by letting go, becoming empty, that we make room for new and healthier thoughts, behaviors, and people to enter our lives.

As we gather the strength to make positive changes and face the truths in ourselves, it is important to keep in mind that letting go does not mean you have nothing to hold on to. It does mean that your hands and your awareness will be free and open when something else comes along. Letting go is the process by which we empty ourselves of the junk that keeps us stuck in our self-destructive patterns. If we can begin to reassure ourselves that letting go is not a loss but rather an acceptance of opportunity, then we will find the process less frightening. Letting go of our attachment to fear and self-destructiveness is similar to the practice of meditation, which teaches us to observe and let pass, observe and let pass. Letting go means not dwelling in the past. The process challenges us to allow everything without getting too attached to anything.

It is important, however, not to minimize, dismiss, or deny the fact that we feel fear when we face the possibility of establishing new boundaries and shedding old beliefs and behaviors. Fear is an appropriate response to such upheaval. This sort of fear is very different from the neurotic, useless fears that held us hostage in the past. Those old fears led to obsessional thinking, compulsive behavior, and physical ailments. This is not the same fear that was our habit in the past. This is the fear of change, the fear of uncertainty. This fear is appropriate, and it will pass.

Rituals are one way in which people seek to establish and maintain a sense of safety. With celebration and ceremony we can honor the parts of ourselves that we are coaxing into being and mourn the parts we seek to shed. As we give up addictions, compulsions, and self-defeating patterns of thought, we lose parts of ourselves that came into being to protect us even though they wound up hurting us instead. Acknowledging the process of release in a ritualized manner allows us to be fully aware of that which we let go of. A ritual can help keep our attention focused in the present by providing a concrete activity. Otherwise we are likely to look fearfully into the void of the future or longingly into the past, when we were still blissfully wandering around in a fog of denial. A ritual, like a meditation, keep us anchored in the present moment and brings new awareness.

Remember the elaborate boundary ritual Laurie performed in Chapter 3? Her coloring and tearing ritual was an eloquent expression of her need for safety and a protective boundary.

Autism seems to provide exaggerated examples of the use of repetitive ritual in the maintenance of personal safety. I am reminded of Raymond in *Rain Man* and of his intense fascination with detail, orderliness, and routine. Whenever he felt threatened or frightened, he would immediately start in on one of his obsessive ordering rituals. This behavior helped him feel safe, perhaps by creating the illusion of control. Nonautistic people have exactly the same concerns and the same tendencies; it's just that they act them out in more subtle and "socially acceptable" ways. Examples include the woman who obsessively cleans the house after arguing with her husband, the young man who cuts hundreds of tiny slashes into his palm when his girlfriend tells him she wants to break up, and the coed who weighs sixty-seven pounds because she thinks her maturing body is disgusting.

The problem is that for many of us, our soothing rituals, what we turn toward for nurture, are not healthy. They are self-destructive. Instead of truly nurturing ourselves, we wind up damaging ourselves. It may seem at first that eating a chocolate cake will ease the pain of a recent disappointment, but once the cake has been swallowed and long before it has been digested, we are heaping recriminations on ourselves. It starts out simply: our feelings get hurt, we can't tolerate being present with our bad feelings, and we want to make them go away. This is when we turn to our addiction of choice without giving a thought to any other ways of dealing with our bad feelings.

When we are faced with unpleasant circumstances, our rational minds allow us to complain until our tongues fall out and to stockpile resentments while never offering us any creative choices. The alternatives of honest confrontation, stepping back from the intensity of the moment, and setting some limits are simply unavailable. In those moments we are incapable of standing up for ourselves; it appears that we would rather run over ourselves. Complaining is a waste of breath even if it is directed at the appropriate people, which it seldom is. Complaining is a back door approach to getting our needs met that is guaranteed to fail. The hidden agenda is that we want things to be different without having to ask for them to be that way.

Complaining becomes a habit, the damaging ritual with which we surround our disappointment.

If we can learn to establish our boundaries and stand by them, we will lose the fear of asking to have our needs met. We will be strong enough to face the possibility that we could be told "No" and have to ask somewhere else. We will be assured in our ability to restate our needs if what we want has not been provided.

Letting go involves discovering what your self-destructive thoughts and behaviors are, honestly admitting them to yourself, deciding whether you are ready and willing to release them, and finally making the decision to do so. Without honest willingness we will be sentenced to failure and regret. There is a big difference between wanting to do something and being willing to do it. For one thing, wanting takes place in the future while willing takes place in the present. Regret is focusing on the past as a means of ignoring the present. We can keep ourselves stuck in a cycle of addiction by wanting to change some behavior, failing to do so, and then feeling like a miserable failure for not having succeeded. When we intimidate ourselves with past failures and look fearfully into the future, we can avoid dealing with our self-destructive patterns in the present.

Imagine that there is only one time frame—now. If each minute, hour, day, or year that went by was just a collection of now moments, one strung out after the other, then any decision we made would only have to be fulfilled right now. We would never have to look down the road toward the future because it wouldn't exist; only now exists. Looking back with regret, longing, or remorse would also be meaningless because now is the

only time there is. Imagine all the worry, dread, sadness, resentment, sorrow, suffering, apprehension, and
fear that could be put aside if there were only now. We
couldn't sustain our complaining and blaming if all time
were now. It would be impossible to lie to ourselves in
now time because it would be impossible to forget to
keep the promises we have made to ourselves. In now
time our tendencies to procrastinate, linger, and post-
pone would no longer be possible. We would be able to
say "No" to the clamor of the internal voices that don't
like to be in now time. If all time were now, it would
not be so easy for the wise, self-preserving part of ourselves to remain a stranger to the addicted, self-
destructive part. The two could come together and help
us create new and healthier rituals.

If you think of ritual in terms of repetitive action and
let your mind be as creative as it knows how to be, you
will be able to come up with a ritual that works for you.
Keep in mind that this ritual should have no self-
destructive elements. Ceremonial dances are the way in
which many cultures act out the events that fill their
lives. Storytelling and myth are other forms of ritual
through which people work our their inner turmoil.
Meditation is a ritual practiced by many people, and it
takes many different forms. Playing a piano can be a
meditation if the correct use of attention is brought to
the activity. If you can open the channels of communication to your intuition, perhaps through your dreams or
by carefully noticing what you are attracted to, you will
devise the sort of ritual you need.

Journal keeping is my consistent ritual of choice. My
journal is the place where I routinely check in with my-

self, where I shed the facade of my personality and attempt to contact the greater wisdom of my soul. The soul is the core of our being, our connection with spirituality, and our most positive and purposeful aspect. The personality, on the other hand, is merely a tool the soul uses in order to function in the physical world. Just as the body is a vehicle for the soul, the personality is a diplomat sent out into the world for the purpose of negotiation. If the soul and the personality are at odds, which is often the case, healing work is required to bring them into better alignment. Without this alignment we are doomed to a cycle of anger, deprivation, and self-destruction. With a proper alignment we approach love, health, and constructive action. Gary Zukav stated in his book *The Seat of the Soul*, "The conflicts of a human's life are directly proportional to the distance at which an energy of personality exists separately from the soul."[1]

Inside the journal is a place where I can most consistently maintain a posture of reverence, where I can risk showing my vulnerability and facing my imperfections. A journal is a place where much self-discovery, honesty, and healing can take place. For me, keeping a regular account of my inner thoughts and outward relations is a healing ritual. There is no time separate from now within the covers of a journal.

For those of us who tend to be highly self-critical and find it difficult to stop comparing ourselves with others, a journal provides a record to which we can refer, sort of like a report card. By looking back we can see our progress and give ourselves credit where it is due rather than measuring ourselves against unattainable or imaginary outcomes. The process of self-negotiation and self-change is supported by the ritual of record keeping.

The final phase of letting go involves making an informed decision. Deciding to let go of things without specifically defining those things and without examining the hidden payoffs for continuing to hold on to them is a setup for failure. We must deliberately decide in what ways we wish change and then establish boundaries that honor our evolving self. Often we think that we really want to diet, quit smoking, or start saving money, but lurking behind the scenes are attitudes that prevent us from successfully making and keeping to our decisions. Each time we betray ourselves, it gets harder to trust. As long as we hold on to attitudes from the past, we are powerless to make changes in the present. To use the metaphor of meditation again, watching our thoughts and attitudes without judging and controlling them will enable us to become aware of where our attention could most fruitfully be directed.

ARROGANCE AND REVERENCE

Reverence is the attitude of honoring all life. It describes a way of behaving that respects the sacredness of all things. Through an attitude of reverence we are connected to everything on the planet at the level of spirit. More powerful than respect, reverence is comprehensive and compassionate. We cannot revere one person or thing without revering all people or things. The practice of reverence leaves behind the personality's need to categorize and judge and focuses attention on purpose, spirituality, and acceptance. Once we have achieved this state, we are no longer threatened by the differences between people, no longer judge ourselves and others harshly, and no longer lie and share only the ideal parts of ourselves. Self-acceptance is a building block for interacting honestly with other people. Once we can accept ourselves, we can accept others and rejoice in the diversity that exists. When we can celebrate differences, we no longer need to fear displeasing others. Right and wrong begin to fade into a gentler tone of "different."

Reverence is compassionate acceptance and, as such, is the antidote to self-hatred. All thoughts, feelings, moods, insights, and actions serve the good of the authentic self and the well-being of all things when they are guided by reverence. Reverence is also an antidote for competition and comparison. Experiencing and celebrating the differences between people, cultures, and ways of interacting can increase the possibilities for peaceful coexistence. No one has to be better than, smarter than, quicker than, or more heavily armed than another, or be the winner when differences are cherished.

By increasing our attention, broadening our awareness, and growing in our reverence, we begin to treat ourselves and others with more love and learn how to stop our self-destructiveness. As our defenses come down and our fears subside, we start experiencing people not as threats or saviors but as vulnerable human beings just like ourselves. Reverence enhances our spirituality and brings with it more patience and understanding. When we operate from a place of reverence, we are able to come out from behind our self-protective barricades and allow people within our boundaries.

Vulnerability is the ability and willingness to be wounded. Becoming vulnerable requires us to accept the risk of being wounded. Consequently, many of us who have been wounded do not wish to take the risk again. Unfortunately, until we are willing to accept the risk of being hurt, we will remain unable to connect with other people. We will continue to erect barriers to communication and interaction because we are still afraid.

As we face the frightening prospect of becoming vulnerable, it is useful to examine the concept of wounding. Surely it means being hurt, but does it necessarily mean being permanently damaged? Many of us were terribly hurt and subsequently damaged as children. We were children, completely without defense, and the damage that resulted has evolved over a lifetime. We have developed intricate defenses, built walls, taken hostages, and medicated our feelings with self-destructiveness.

This book is a guidebook for discovering and healing previously damaged parts of ourselves so that we can stop self-administering pain. When we are conscious of our decision to be vulnerable or invulnerable, we have choice. When we are afraid, there is no choice. The pain, hurt, and disappointment that may come our way as a result of increased vulnerability will be met with the capabilities of an adult. We are no longer the dependent, trusting child who was hurt by an abusive, intrusive, overprotective, critical, or enmeshed parent. We are far more resourceful than that. Remember hearing

"This hurts me more than it does you" as you were being punished? It wasn't the truth—it hurt you more, both physically and psychically.

Arrogance is the reverse of reverence and a major distraction from the process of shedding self-destructiveness. Arrogance will always convince us of our ultimate rightness even in the face of the threat of self-demise. Addicts and alcoholics are typically the most arrogant people you are likely to meet. Arrogance is their defense, their armor against self-honesty, and their barrier to self-respect. Arrogance is what we must let go of.

Arrogance is an exaggeration of one's own worth and superiority. Ironically, arrogance can often be found in those of us with the lowest self-esteem. Under its spell it is impossible to humble oneself to the point of being able to acknowledge a power greater than oneself. Arrogance is a tremendous barrier to establishing an honest relationship with the self or the other. It is a defense mechanism that keeps people at a distance and is responsible for much of the destructiveness in the world. No one would start a war, kill another human being, or deliberately pollute a river unless he was able to convince himself of the moral necessity of such an action. This is arrogance at its most dangerous.

An arrogant attitude makes peer relationships impossible because superiority is always inherent. People with poor boundaries and low self-esteem are often attracted to arrogant people, mistaking their bluster for an honest sense of self-worth. These people are attracted to the apparent strength and assurance the arrogant person exudes, hoping perhaps that some of it will rub off. Instead, what often happens as the friendship or relationship continues is that the arrogant person begins to resent the adoring eye of the other and starts turning arrogant disdain in that person's direction. People with healthy boundaries need not resort to arrogance. When we don't feel threatened by everything and everybody, we are able to be reverent.

RESENTMENT AND FORGIVENESS

Resentment is a feeling of indignant displeasure or persistent ill will directed at something we regard as wrong. The affront can be an insult, a slight, a lie, an omission, a betrayal, a direct physical injury, or merely a disappointed expectation. Whatever the stimulus, resentment is a response of anger and self-righteousness. Anger in and of itself may be the entirely correct and understandable response to the offending action. The problem arises when anger is joined by self-righteousness. When we combine the two, it is difficult to work through and release our feelings of anger, leaving us with this persistent ill will: resentment. Self-righteousness is a false boundary behind which we hide our true selves and true feelings. Surrounding oneself with self-righteousness is a way to remain disconnected from other people, a way to feel superior.

Constant ruminating, replaying conversations, reviewing unpleasant interactions in our minds, and retelling our stories of outrage to anyone who will listen are some of the addictive maneuvers of resentment. Unless we can keep the coals of our anger alive through continuous complaint, resentment will die and we will lose our self-righteous high. This behavior has all the characteristics of an addiction.

In some cases arrogance and resentful outrage are insufficient medications against feelings of hurt and disappointment. Some people have such difficulty expressing their feelings honestly or confronting other people that they resort to revenge as the only means of discharging unpleasant feelings. Their belief seems to be that the best way to stop feeling pain is to inflict some. Revenge is the opposite of reverence.

Resentment is connected to our tendency to rely too heavily on our expectations. When we are unable to accept what is as what is, we are left locked in a realm of disappointment and resentment. Impossible standards, unreal goals, and exorbitant expectations make it difficult to experience present reality. Our focus is always attached to the illusion we project into the future. We live on a roller coaster of anticipation of the future and disappointment at the past, once more avoiding the present moment.

The word *should* is a clue to noticing when we are expecting and anticipating. Illusions tell us what the world should be like and how we should feel. When we participate in this fantasy, we wind up feeling continually abused by an uncaring world or end up believing that there is something very flawed within us. *Should* is presumptuous and constitutes a spiritual boundary violation. Who is to say that what is isn't exactly the way it is supposed to be?

Forgiveness is the antidote for feelings of resentment. Forgiveness is the attitude that can fill the void when we truly let go of persistent ill will. Forgiving is sometimes held up in front of people as a "should." Whenever this has been done, forgiveness has been used as an instrument for violating boundaries. Forgiveness has its own time schedule, and no one has the right to push anyone else toward it.

Parents and organized religions collude in filling people with guilt over the issue of forgiveness. Strict religious doctrine tends to boil down the mysteries and questions of life into a manageable broth of rigid values and absolute truths. Parental dictates and religious commandments state how one should feel and behave.

Trying to follow the external mandate to forgive has resulted in a tremendous amount of confusion, guilt, resentment, and lying. First people are urged to believe or threatened into believing that they should forgive. But they are given little information about what the process of forgiveness involves. Does forgiveness mean that no matter how many times you were beaten as a child, it was all right because your parents really loved you? Or does it mean that even though your mother read all your diaries and then made you explain why you had written them, you forgive her because she was just being a good mother? Or does it mean that even though your husband had an affair with your best friend, you forgive both of them because it is over? These possibilities and countless others that have been shared throughout this book are examples of boundary violations. Physical, emotional, spiritual, and intellectual boundaries are violated in countless ways, but instead of acknowledging this reality, we urge people to ignore their feelings and forgive. Forcing oneself to rush dutifully and piously into forgiveness is an act of self-harm. This is why it is so important to understand something about this issue.

One of the confusions that haunts many people about forgiveness is its association with forgetting. The two are often linked—"Forgive and forget"—and they become dangerously blended. To forgive does not require that we forget, and this is extremely important to keep in mind. The parts of us that have been damaged don't want to feel forgotten, abandoned, and uncared for. Therefore, to ask and expect ourselves to forget is just another insulting request for reality to be erased. No wonder we would rather stubbornly hold on to the self-damaging resentments we carry than risk annihilation through forgetting. Before we can hope to begin cultivating forgiveness in our hearts, we must separate that concept from forgetting.

Forgetting is not a requirement for forgiving, but forgiving does require that we release the past and turn our attention to the present. The process is the same whether we are forgiving other people or forgiving ourselves. Forgiving does not require that we deny that whatever has happened hurt, frightened, or disappointed us in some way, but it does require that we set down the weight of those feelings and breathe a sigh of relief. Once we can honestly release our resentments, we no longer need to consume so much energy holding on to them.

If the urge to wound ourselves is tied up with the past and with misdirected attempts to reconnect with that time and those feelings, then turning our complete attention to the present can help diminish our self-destructiveness.

JUDGING AND FORGIVENESS

Judging ourselves and others places us in unbalanced relationships. It is impossible to be internally balanced or self-centered when we are engaged in judging ourselves. To be involved in the act of judging we must step outside ourselves and become observers. Whenever we do this, we lose our balance, our integration. We may be focusing on our ideal selves, our imaginary perfect selves, and beating ourselves up mentally for being who we actually are. Or we may be allowing our internal dialogue to get wrapped up with our inner critic. Whatever the impetus, when we are engaged in judging ourselves, we have snuck behind enemy lines and handed ourselves over as a hostage. As prisoners we can only hope that the future will bring rescue or lament the past that brought us to this state. We will be distracted from the present moment by the ruminations of our minds, and the truth about ourselves will be obscured.

Judging other people, as I have mentioned, develops as an automatic adaptation within a culture that trains us to compete. Our boundaries become so weakened in this environment that unless we are assessing other people, judging them, and ranking ourselves in comparison, the simple act of being present with people may make us feel that we are evaporating.

Insecurity is the primary motivation for the activity of judging people. Some would argue that judging is a skill needed for the delicate art of discerning the character of other people. These people would say that judging others is an act of self-protection. But if this were true, prejudice would have a better reputation. As it stands, critically judging other people is motivated by our own feelings of inferiority. As we begin to let go of our need to judge ourselves and others, our sense of self starts to heal.

Forgiveness is the process of finding and reclaiming our innermost trust. As we become willing to let go of our obsessive need to dwell and fester in the past and as we let go of the fear that seeks to control uncertainty, we begin to allow for a natural flow in our lives. Getting to the point where jumping into the abyss feels safe requires coming to trust ourselves and believing that everything will be perfectly fine if we let go. Trusting is built on a spiritual belief that acknowledges that there are powers greater than ourselves at work. Forgiveness reminds us that we are not responsible for the workings of the universe.

Forgiveness also involves learning to appreciate and honor the differences between people. Healing through forgiveness does not mean achieving consensus; the point is to accept divergence. Each and every person is a unique individual with his own particular history and lessons to learn. We pay lip service to individuality, but in the end we really don't appreciate a very wide range of diversity. We are quick to negatively label and criticize individuality that diverges too much from our expectations. An attitude of forgiveness reminds us of the spirituality of individuals and our separate journeys on this planet. Forgiveness allows us to truly embrace differences rather than continue judging and criticizing them.

OVERPROTECTION AND RESPECT

When we can release our obsessive need to control people and protect them from the full experience of their lives, we can begin to honestly love and respect them.

A child who grows up in a home filled with respect and compassion is encouraged to explore and experiment within the bounds of his experience and ability. Parents create the boundaries of safety and modify them as the child grows. The child does not fear recrimination from the parents for making mistakes. He is not afraid of being abandoned for small slipups. He feels free to learn, and what he learns is that the world is an uncontrollable, unexpected, and confusing place. This child has been lovingly prepared for the reality of life.

A child who grows up under strict, dogmatic parents may be well behaved, but this child is not well prepared for adult life. Typically these are the children who, the moment they are let out of the house, start engaging in risk taking and self-destructive behavior with a vengeance. Instead of protecting their children, their parents have programmed them for early destruction. Kids like this are riveted on the future. "I can't wait until I go away to college" and "When I'm eighteen, I'm moving out and then you can't tell me what to do" are phrases commonly spoken by kids who suffer too much protection and parental authority.

There are people, not only parents, who need to control the safety and predictability of all events. They strive to avoid confrontation at all costs and are led to overprotecting other people. Here, too, we have the problem of attention not being focused in the present. Instead, concentration is projected onto a fearful future filled with threat. This fear of the future and a complete lack of confidence in the competence of other people lead overprotecting people to try to control everything. By imagining that we are operating out of a concern for another person's feelings, we convince ourselves of our righteousness and remain in denial about the truth.

Respect requires restraint from interfering with the object of our respect. Interference includes imagining what others will think of us if we tell them how we really feel. It involves what we tell ourselves others will say if we stand up and show our true vulnerability. Interfering involves any activity, conscious or otherwise, that obscures authenticity. Respect for others is no different from respect for the self. Respecting ourselves allows us to set healthy boundaries, and respect for others assures us that they will handle the changes in their lives on their own without the need for our unsolicited assistance.

COMPARISON AND SELF-RESPECT

Self-respect involves moving into present reality and accepting what is there. This acceptance does not preclude improvement, but as long as we mentally bash ourselves with our real or imagined defects, we damage ourselves.

We can never know exactly what goes on inside other people's minds, but we assume that we do know when we compare ourselves with other people. We imagine that they have all the answers, the self-confidence, the brains that we do not. The beautiful man or woman, perfectly dressed, with a fine car and other material amenities, may appear happy, confident, whatever it is we desire, but we can never know if our assumptions are correct. So why, with all this uncertainty, do we choose to insult ourselves by unfavorably comparing ourselves with anyone else?

Similarly, the pages of magazines are filled with images of people younger, prettier, and smarter, and they all have the benefit of a talented artistic staff and our imaginations to become even more appealing. If we could turn our awareness to the comforting reality that we are not models and remember that we are probably not eighteen years old anymore, we might be gentler in our self-assessment. Until we can shed the harsh critic of comparison, we cannot hope to maintain a shred of self-respect.

Comparison is longing for the past or gazing wishfully into the future. If we could be conscious in the present, we would not unconsciously hurt ourselves in the ways we do.

Self-respect is movement back toward our center. It is an attitude of valuing ourselves in a way that does not permit damaging thoughts and behavior to intrude. When we operate with a genuine sense of self-respect, we are capable of maintaining healthy boundaries with ease. Respect for the self brings with it respect for others and allows for the development of mutual communication and satisfying relationships. When we respect ourselves, we can also honestly accept all aspects of ourselves, especially our broken parts. When we can accept our imperfections, we can share them with other people and be vulnerable. Through this sharing and trusting we authentically connect with other people. This is how we come out of the isolation and self-destructiveness of our fear.

We are all on a journey, a path, a healing quest, a spiritual awakening—whatever you want to call it. Once we become aware of this journey, we can stop struggling against it and begin cooperating with the magical process of growth and learning. To surrender to this process we must release the expectations and judgments that separate us from ourselves and other people. We must let go of our tendency to escape from our feelings with a quick fix. It is necessary to confront and examine our compulsive and addictive patterns—not to condemn ourselves for having them but to honestly acknowledge and accept them. As long as we remain trapped by the need to control, compete, compare, and dominate, we will not be able to release our will over to a power greater than the self.

In spite of our valiant struggles, we are powerless to change much in our lives until we change what is in our minds. We can change jobs and partners, we can move, and we can rearrange the furniture, but unless we work on the inside, nothing really is any different. We are capable of changing the climate of our minds by becoming careful observers. When we stumble around mindlessly, we hurt ourselves, but when we become mindful and aware, we are able to make informed choices and introduce beneficial changes into our lives. As Hamlet so knowingly stated, "There is nothing either good or bad, but thinking makes it so."

Becoming mindful increases our awareness and allows us to take more risks. We lose our fear of failure because the concept of failure loses its meaning. Our limitations begin to fall away as we turn our attention toward them for closer examination. Self-scrutiny is a prerequisite for healthy self-maintenance.

COMING BACK TO CENTER

For all the reasons discussed in this book and probably many others, people reach adulthood with damaged boundaries. They are out of touch with their internal needs and feelings and are incapable of honestly connecting with other people. They are hurling rubber balls at one another and taking one another prisoner. The prisoners are helplessly waiting to be rescued. It's a game, but few people are having much fun.

Coming back to center or becoming self-centered and in balance is how we can stop participating in the game of bombardment and begin connecting in a gentler way with ourselves and other people. One of the first steps is to let go of who we think we are supposed to be. If we can stop judging ourselves at every turn, we can begin to relax and let other people see us as we truly are. When we can accept ourselves, we are less inclined to automatically accept the premise of other people and are able to respect and protect our boundaries. When we don't accept ourselves, we cannot trust ourselves, and if we do not trust, we cannot hope to let go of our need to control.

A deeply buried and socially reinforced sense of unworthiness is another shackle on self-esteem that needs to be released in order for us to reclaim self-acceptance and love. It is this veil of unworthiness that convinces us that we'll lose our jobs if we ask for a raise or will lose a friend if we tell him how we really feel. Unworthiness lurks behind our internal censors, telling us we'll be thought of as bad if we stand up for ourselves and honor our boundaries. The words *distrust* and *destruct* share more than similar spelling. It is crucial that we find a way to regain a basic sense of trust in ourselves and shed the conditioning of our past. Self-trust is the cornerstone for healthy boundaries.

It is precisely because the concept of reclaiming the self-center runs contrary to the cultural perspective of negatively labeling self-centeredness that I have chosen to view it in a completely different context. Healing our damaged boundaries requires us to cultivate our ability to engage in introspection, to turn our attention inward. It also involves learning to ask questions and form our own opinions. Once those opinions have been formed, we must trust ourselves to share them even if they are different from what other people think. Differences do not indicate rightness or wrongness unless we define them as such. Without clear boundaries, we fear that differences indicate conflict. Within boundaries, differences can be easily accepted for what they are— dissimilar expressions of unique individuals. As we grow in our ability to accept differences, we can extend ourselves and become involved with more people. We no longer need to hide.

Once we have reestablished center, we may find that we are no longer compulsively driven to connect with other people. We will not need other people to make us feel better about ourselves. It may be that we have to develop some specific training exercise, like the one I shared in Chapter 3, that will allow us to be less prompt in our response to other people's real or imagined requests. The following is a list of some ideas and hints I have found helpful on my learning journey.

GUIDELINES FOR SETTING BOUNDARIES
- There is no perfect limit.
- A boundary depends on the person and the situation.
- Boundaries can change depending on the situation or your feelings.

TRY THESE EXERCISES AS YOU BEGIN TO ESTABLISH BOUNDARIES

Say "No" at least twice a day.

Find words and phrases other than "No" that mean what you want to say. (This will provide safety until you can release the idea that "No" means "I don't like you.")

Take up more room than you usually would.

Become a curious observer, rather than a harsh critic, of yourself.

Confront that which scares you. Meet your fears and make friends.

Learn to tolerate ambiguity and uncertainty.

Pay attention.

Do one thing at a time.

Be in the moment.

Be kind to yourself.

Be flexible. It's hard to be disappointed that way. But when you are disappointed, pay attention. Disappointment can show us the limits of reality.

Don't read other people's minds; keep your attention on yourself. Be aware of others.

Discard the myth of the quick fix. Consider the price being paid for immediate gratification.

Stop trying to manage outcomes. Live in the moment and see what happens.

You might want to write down any of the ideas or phrases in this book that have been meaningful or that have made an impression on you, the ones that hold the most energy for you. These are the phrases that make your skin prickle or your heart beat faster, the ones that make you feel more hopeful and powerful. Write them down and carry them around with you like a credit card. Our minds have a tendency to revert to old thoughts and behaviors when under stress. Therefore, having some helpful reminders to strengthen our efforts can be extremely useful.

Transformation takes place when we can acknowledge hidden and denied aspects of ourselves, name them, and give them space in our awareness. Self-harm takes place when we continue to hide and deny. Until we acknowledge our problems, we remain trapped by them. Once we honestly look at ourselves, we know what we have to work with.

It is my sincere hope that as people learn to honor the

sacredness of personal boundaries, they will begin connecting with greater honesty and love. When we feel safe and secure, it is hard to imagine the need to lash out and attack ourselves or others. As we cleanse ourselves of self-destructiveness, we contribute less to the world's destructiveness.

Be at peace.

Notes

CHAPTER 1

1. Ashley Montagu, *Touching: The Human Significance of the Skin* (New York: Harper & Row, 1971).
2. Richard D'Ambrosio, M.D., *No Language but a Cry* (Garden City, N.Y.: Doubleday, 1970).

CHAPTER 2

1. Shakti Gawain, *Return to the Garden* (San Rafael, Calif.: New World Library, 1989).
2. Kim Chernin, *The Obsession: Reflections on the Tyranny of Slenderness* (New York: Harper Colophon, 1981).
3. Robert Seidenberg and Karen DeCrow, *Women Who Marry Houses* (New York: McGraw-Hill, 1983), 169.
4. Barent W. Walsh and Paul M. Rosen, *Self-Mutilation: Theory, Research, and Treatment* (New York: Guilford Press, 1988).
5. Ibid.
6. Bruno Bettelheim, *The Empty Fortress: Infantile Autism and the Birth of the Self* (New York: Free Press, 1967), 137.

233

7. Alice Miller, *Banished Knowledge: Facing Childhood Injuries* (Garden City, N.Y.: Doubleday, 1990).

CHAPTER 3

1. Bob Marsenich, *Ready, Aim, Change: A Toolbook for Managing Personal Change* (Pawleys Island, S.C.: Seaglass Publications, 1989).
2. Bettelheim, op. cit.

CHAPTER 4

1. Maggie Scarf, *Intimate Partners: Patterns in Love and Marriage* (New York: Random House, 1987).
2. Deborah Tannen, Ph.D., *You Just Don't Understand: Men and Women in Conversation* (New York: William Morrow, 1990).
3. Alfie Kohn, *No Contest: The Case against Competition* (Boston: Houghton Mifflin, 1986).
4. Scarf, op. cit.

CHAPTER 5

1. Miller, op. cit.
2. Ibid.
3. Taj Mahal, "Cakewalk into Town," Big Toot Tunes, EMI Blackwood Music, 1972.

CHAPTER 6

1. John Bradshaw, *Healing the Shame That Binds You* (Deerfield Beach, Fla.: Health Communications, 1988).
2. Arnold Madison, *Suicide and Young People* (New York: Clarion Books, 1978).
3. Frederick Henry Smith, *Nail-Biting: The Beatable Habit* (Provo, Utah: Brigham Young University Press, 1980).
4. Walsh and Rosen, op. cit.
5. Stephen Levine, *A Gradual Awakening* (Garden City, N.Y.: Doubleday, 1989).
6. Anne Wilson Schaef, *When Society Becomes an Addict* (San Francisco: Harper & Row, 1987).

CHAPTER 7

1. Gary Zukav, *The Seat of the Soul* (New York: Simon & Schuster, 1989).

Bibliography

Adair, Margot. *Working Inside Out*. Berkeley, Calif.: Wingbow Press, 1984.

Bass, Ellen, and Laura Davis. *The Courage to Heal: A Guild for Women Survivors of Child Sexual Abuse*. New York: Harper & Row, 1988.

Bettelheim, Bruno. *The Empty Fortress: Infantile Autism and the Birth of the Self*. New York: Free Press, 1967.

Borysenko, Joan, Ph.D. *Guilt Is the Teacher, Love Is the Lesson*. New York: Warner Books, 1990.

Bowan-Woodward, Kathy, Ph.D. *Coping with a Negative Body Image*. New York: Rosen, 1989.

Bowlby, John. *Attachment and Loss*. New York: Basic Books, 1969.

Bradshaw, John. *Healing the Shame That Binds You*. Deerfield Beach, Fla.: Health Communications, 1988.

Brandt, David, Ph.D. *Is That All There Is? Overcoming Disappointment in an Age of Diminished Expectations*. New York: Poseidon Press, 1984.

Bruch, Hilde, M.D. *The Golden Cage: The Enigma of Anorexia Nervosa*. New York: Vintage Books, 1978.

Bruch, Hilde, M.D. *Conversations with Anorexics*. New York: Basic Books, 1988.

Bruner, Jerome, and Helen Haste. *Making Sense*. New York: Methuen, 1987.

Chernin, Kim. *The Obsession: Reflections on the Tyranny of Slenderness*. New York: Harper Colophon, 1981.

Covitz, Joel. *Emotional Child Abuse: The Family Curse*. Boston: Sigo Press, 1986.

D'Ambrosio, Richard, M.D. *No Language but a Cry*. Garden City, N.Y: Doubleday, 1970.

Ginott, Haim G., M.D. *Between Parent and Child: New Solutions to Old Problems*. New York: Macmillan, 1965.

Goleman, Daniel. *Vital Lies, Simple Truths: The Psychology of Self-Deception*. New York: Simon & Schuster, 1985.

Hempe, Ruth S., and C. Henry. *Child Abuse*. Cambridge, Mass.: Harvard University Press, 1978.

Hodgson, Ray and Peter Miller. *SelfWatching: Addictions, Habits, Compulsions: What to Do about Them*. New York: Facts on File, 1982.

Kiley, John Cantwell, M.D., Ph.D. *Self-Rescue*. Portland, Ore.: Metamorphous Press, 1990.

Kohn, Alfie. *No Contest: The Case against Competition*. Boston: Houghton Mifflin, 1986.

Langer, Ellen J. *Mindfulness*. Reading, Mass.: Addison-Wesley, 1989.

Levine, Stephen. *A Gradual Awakening*. Garden City, N.Y.: Doubleday, 1989.

Madison, Arnold. *Suicide and Young People*. New York: Clarion Books, 1978.

Marsenich, Bob. *Ready, Aim, Change: A Toolbook for*

Managing Personal Change. Pawleys Island, S.C.: Seaglass Publications, 1989.

Middleton-Moz, Jane, and Lorie Dwinell. *After the Tears.* Pompano Beach, Fla.: Health Communications, 1986.

Milkman, Harvey and Stanley Sunderwirth. *Craving for Ecstasy: The Consciousness and Chemistry of Escape.* Lexington, Mass.: Lexington Books, 1987.

Miller, Alice. *Banished Knowledge: Facing Childhood Injuries.* New York: Doubleday, 1990.

Minuchin, Salvador, Bernice L. Rosman and Lester Baker. *Psychosomatic Families: Anorexia Nervosa in Context.* Cambridge, Mass.: Harvard University Press, 1978.

Montagu, Ashley. *Touching: The Human Significance of the Skin.* New York: Harper & Row, 1971.

Montagu, Ashley, and Floyd Matson. *The Dehumanization of Man.* New York: McGraw-Hill, 1983.

Parker, Rolland S., Ph.D. *Emotional Common Sense.* New York: Harper & Row, 1981.

Peck, M. Scott, M.D. *The Different Drum: Community-Making and Peace.* New York: Simon & Schuster, 1987.

Rubin, Theodore Isaac, M.D. *Compassion and Self-Hate: An Alternative to Despair.* New York: Collier Books, 1975.

Rumney, Avis. *Dying to Please: Anorexia Nervosa and Its Cure.* Jefferson, N.C.: McFarland, 1983.

Scarf, Maggie. *Intimate Partners: Patterns in Love and Marriage.* New York: Random House, 1987.

Schaef, Anne Wilson. *When Society Becomes an Addict.* San Francisco: Harper & Row, 1987.

Seidenberg, Robert and Karen DeCrow. *Women Who Marry Houses*. New York: McGraw-Hill, 1983.

Shainess, Natalie, M.D. *Sweet Suffering: Woman as Victim*. Indianapolis: Bobbs-Merrill, 1984.

Smith, Frederick Henry. *Nail-Biting: The Beatable Habit*. Provo, Utah: Brigham Young University Press, 1980.

Tannen, Deborah, Ph.D. *You Just Don't Understand: Women and Men in Conversation*. New York: William Morrow, 1990.

Walsh, Barent W., and Paul M. Rosen. *Self-Mutilation: Theory, Research, & Treatment*. New York: Guilford Press, 1988.

Weinberg, George. *The Pliant Animal*. New York: St. Martin's Press, 1981.

Wills-Brandon, Carla. *Learning to Say No: Establishing Healthy Boundaries*. Deerfield Beach, Fla.: Health Communications, 1990.

Wolpe, Joseph, M.D., and David Wolpe. *Our Useless Fears*. Boston: Houghton Mifflin, 1981.

Zukav, Gary. *The Seat of the Soul*. New York: Simon & Schuster, 1989.